The Honey Book

Instrumento per le Api

The Honey Book

by LUCILLE RECHT PENNER

Illustrated with photographs and old prints
arranged by Ronnie Ann Herman

HASTINGS HOUSE, *Publishers* NEW YORK

Library of Congress Cataloging in Publication Data

Penner, Lucille Recht   The honey book.

    Bibliography: p.
    Includes index.
    SUMMARY: An introduction to the importance of honey throughout history and around the world, including discussions of its composition and how it is produced, gathered, sold, and used. Includes a number of recipes for cosmetics and food dishes.
    1. Honey—Juvenile literature. 2. Cookery (Honey)—Juvenile literature. 3. Bee culture—Juvenile literature. [1. Honey. 2. Cookery—Honey. 3. Bee Culture] I. Title.
SF539.P45   1980   641.3'8   80-249

ISBN 0-8038-3054-8

Published simultaneously in Canada by
Saunders of Toronto, Ltd., Don Mills, Ontario
Printed in the United States of America

Contents

THE ANCIENT WORLD
Pasteli (*Greek Sesame Seed Candy*) • Honeyed Cheesecakes •
Panchamrit (*Yogurt Drink*) • Roman Dates • Peas à la
Vitellius (*Peas in an Egg Sauce*)

[5]

THE MIDDLE AGES

Golden Apples • Rysbred (*Rice Pancakes*) • Douce Âme (*Capon in Milk and Honey*) • Frumenty (*Wheat Pudding*) • Nurembergers (*Honey Cookies*) • Cameline Sauce

AROUND THE WORLD

Scottish Honey Scones • Bircher Muesli (*Swiss Cereal*) • Mehalis (*Orange Rice*) • Oen Cymreig Melog (*Welsh Honeyed Lamb*) • Tzimmes (*Meat and Vegetable Stew*) • Genoese Chestnut Hot Pot • Arabian Chicken • Sweet and Sour Spareribs • Spiced Acorn Squash • Brazilian Yogurt Cream • Csalla Mary (*Hungarian Salad*) • Honey Glazed Carrots • Charoses (*Apple-Nut Relish*) • Honeyed Nahit (*Baked Chickpeas*) • Candied Orange or Lemon Peel • Rose Honey • Russian Beet Jam • Fig Bread • Oatcakes • Pain d'Épices (*Honey Bread*) • Scripture Cake • Honey Jumbles (*Cookies*) • Honey Bran Muffins • Lekach (*Honey Cake*) • Algerian Charlotte • Scandinavian Fruit Soup • Honey Custard • Peanut Butter Balls • Honey Icing • Meli Pita (*Honey Pie*) • Aish-el Saraya (*Egyptian Palace Bread*) • Fruit Compote • Spicy Oranges

Recipes

[7]

Acknowledgments

I am grateful for the help given me by editors, librarians, and friends. Lawrence Goltz, Editor of *Gleanings in Bee Culture*, reviewed the manuscript and generously advised me on questions related to bees and beekeeping. Dr. Eva Crane, Editor of *Bee World*, provided many wonderful prints and photographs from the files of the International Bee Research Association and from her own collection. Miss C. L. Dickson of the Moir Beekeeping Library kindly assisted my research in Edinburgh, and the Edinburgh City Library was extremely generous in providing illustrations from its collection. I am grateful, too, to have had access to the splendid picture collection of the New York Public Library.

The California Honey Advisory Board gave me permission to use the recipes for fig bread and honey custard. Mrs. Pushpa Gupta of the Information Service of India contributed the recipe for *Panchamrit*. The Embassy of Israel provided the recipe for *Lekach*. The recipes for Brazilian

[9]

Cream, Genoese Chestnut Hot Pot, and *Csalla Mary* are reproduced from *Honey Cookery* by Chris Stadtlaender, by kind permission of Thorsons Publishers, Ltd. George Braziller, Inc. gave permission for the use of recipes—from *Fabulous Feasts*, by Madeline Cosman—for Rysbred and Golden Apples.

I should also like to thank Edward Weiss for an education in beekeeping and for showing me his apiary in Connecticut. I am grateful to Lawrence and Maureen Dennis, of Carbondale, Illinois, for allowing me to participate in harvesting honey from their hives. Special thanks to John and Audrey Stenton whose help and hospitality were invaluable during my research in England.

Finally, I should like to thank my editor, Judy Donnelly, and her assistant, Elise Berkower, for their commitment to this book, their painstaking work, and their unending care.

PICTURE ACKNOWLEDGMENTS: Bibliotheque Nationale, Paris, 76; Bodleian Library, Oxford, 48; Cambridge University Library, 72; International Bee Research Association, 37, 42, 45, 70, 79, 132, 135; Kupferstichkabinett, Staatliche Museen Preussicher, Kulturbesitz, Berlin (West), 50-51; Photo courtesy Library of Congress, 16; The Metropolitan Museum of Art, Harris Brisbane Dick Fund, 1926, 105; The Metropolitan Museum of Art, Rogers Fund, 1919, 106; Mouffet's *Theatre of Insects*, 1934, 88, 119, 130; Musée de Strasbourg, 94; Museum Boymans-van Beuningen, Rotterdam, 108-109; Courtesy Museum of Fine Arts, Boston, Bequest of Charles B. Hoyt, 123; Courtesy the New York Historical Society, 91; The New York Public Library Picture Collection, 2, 14, 17, 19, 23, 24, 25, 26, 33, 44, 53, 54, 55, 56, 61, 65, 68, 84, 85, 86, 92, 93, 97, 101, 114, 115, 120, 124, 126, 130, 137, 139, 144, 146, 148-149, 150; Rare Book Division, The New York Public Library, Astor, Lenox, and Tilden Foundations, 66-67; Courtesy of the A. I. Root Company, 12, 34; By courtesy of the Scottish Beekeepers Association, 29, 38, 40, 47, 112, 113, 140; University of Arizona Library, Courtesy of SPECIAL COLLECTIONS, 30, 74, 75, 90, 99, 103, 104, 110, 118, 122, 128-129, 142; U.S.D.A. Photographs, 28, 59, 64; State of Utah, Dept. of Development Services, 82.

Illustrations arranged by Ronnie Ann Herman.

To my mother, Adele Klein Recht,
and my aunt, Doris Klein Elfenbein

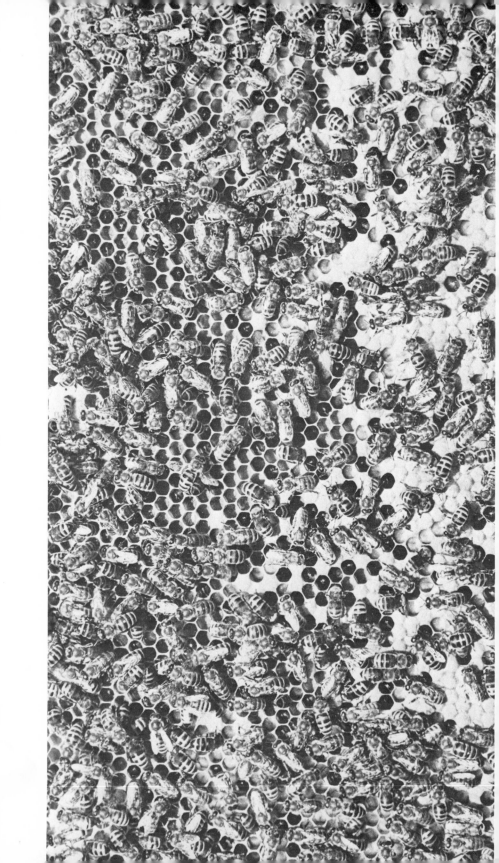

CHAPTER ONE

Surprising Honey

A drop of honey catches more flies than
a barrel of vinegar.
—Old Proverb

HONEY is one of the most remarkable foods in the world. It can be eaten with no preparation at all. It does not have to be cooked, processed, or blended with other ingredients.

If honey is sealed and stored in a dry place, it will keep for years—even centuries—without any preservatives. In fact, honey itself is a preservative.

In addition to its obvious qualities—sweetness and stickiness—honey has some special properties of which few people are aware. Honey is *hygroscopic*. This means that it absorbs moisture—even the moisture in the air around us. So breads and cakes made with honey don't dry out as they age, the way cakes made with sugar do.

Partly because of its hygroscopic quality, honey is also antiseptic—it actually destroys some kinds of bacteria. Like all living things, bacteria need moisture. Honey draws out their moisture and kills them. Furthermore, honey contains hydrogen peroxide, a well-known germ-killer.

The use of honey is older than human civilization. Since earliest times, honey has been sought, even at the risk

of life itself, to use as a medicine, to trade for other valuable
goods, to present as an offering to the gods, and to enliven
the taste of every kind of food and drink. The first part of
this book tells that remarkable story.

In the second part of the book you will find honey recipes from all over the world and from different periods of
history. As you prepare them and enjoy them, you will be
joining a tradition of many centuries, a tradition that
crosses mountains and spans oceans, and unites people of
all races and cultures—the tradition of eating honey.

THE   BEES   WORK-A-DAY   SONG.

" Busy-bee, busy-buzz, buz-a-buz-a-bee-buss !
We're the busiest insects; take lessons from us.
Busy-bee, busy-buzz, buz-a-buz-a-bee-buss !"

CHAPTER TWO

Healthful Honey

Honey is drunk against the biting of a Serpent or mad Dog and it is good for them which have eaten mushrooms or drunk Poppy. . . . It is also good for falling sickness and better than wine because it cannot rise to the head as wine doeth.

—*History of Bees*, Charles Butler, 1623

HONEY certainly tastes good—but is it also especially good *for* you?

Throughout history, many people have been sure that the answer is yes. In fact, at one time or another, in one country or another, honey has been prescribed as a cure or preventive for practically everything. It has been claimed to soothe the nerves, ward off snakebite, cure hayfever, banish insomnia, soothe upset stomachs, relieve aches and pains. It has been used as a laxative. It has been given to lower fever.

Is your hair turning white? The treatment recommended in ancient Assyria was to smear on a paste made from bees roasted in oil. Perhaps things are still worse—you are going completely bald? Galen, a famous Greek physician, suggested applying a paste made of powdered bees and honey to your scalp in order to restore your hair.

Galen had an equally imaginative prescription to

strengthen weak eyesight: four parts of honey mixed with one part of the gall of the sea tortoise.

In ancient China and India, honey was used more for medicinal purposes than for food. Hindus believed that whoever ate honey was likely to become strong, rich, and wise; and also to improve his looks and those of his yet-to-be-born children. Honey was thought to work specific cures depending on the kind of flower from which the bees had gathered their nectar and the time of year the honey was harvested. Elements of these beliefs survive in the folk medicine of India today.

The Arabs, too, believed that honey was an effective medicine. Mohammed is quoted as saying, "Honey is a remedy for every illness and the Koran is a remedy for all illnesses of the mind. Therefore I recommend to you both remedies, the Koran and honey."

In medieval Europe a wide variety of imaginative honey drinks were used to treat diseases. Mixtures of honey and rainwater, honey and vinegar, honey and pepper, or honey and wine were said to cure illnesses such as gout and rheumatism. Here's a recipe for *thalasomel*, a treatment for digestive ailments. It was supposed to cause vomiting, and sounds as though it very well might. "Mix equal parts of seawater, rainwater, and honey. Strain the mixture and place it in a container lined with tar. Expose this to the hot rays of the July sun."

Perhaps strangest of all is the notion that eating honey is an effective treatment for obesity. According to the ancient Greek writer Herodotus, Egyptian women ate honey at breakfast every day to keep their figures trim. It sounds like one of the pleasantest diets ever devised. Of course, our distant ancestors had no way of knowing, as we do today, that honey is extremely fattening.

Hetep, the Egyptian god of medicine.

Though the ancients may have been wrong about some of the powers of honey, much of the old medical lore makes good sense. In ancient times just as today, honey was often recommended as a treatment for hoarseness, coughs, and sore throats. One old prescription calls for a blend of honey, oils, and lemon juice, which must have tasted very much like a modern cough drop. Today, honey is an ingredient in commercial cough syrups and in home remedies for colds.

Because honey does have antiseptic properties, early physicians were right to use it as a dressing for wounds. Even today, medical journals occasionally include reports on the use of honey as a surgical dressing or a treatment for burns. Some doctors have also prescribed honey for hayfever sufferers—they say that honey from the flowers that cause a patient's hayfever will relieve its symptoms. Experiments on the medicinal powers of honey continue all over the world. We may find that still other ancient honey remedies are scientifically sound and effective.

What of honey as a food? Today, many people believe that it is healthier to eat foods that have not been refined or mixed with chemical additives. Honey is a natural food that requires no preservatives or additives and needs no processing. It can be eaten just as it is harvested.

Chemically, honey consists almost entirely of sugar and water—a fact that would seem very odd if you were to boil up some sugar syrup and then compare its thin sweetness with the rich taste of honey. The following chart gives the principal components of honey.

```
Sugars: Levulose ...............  38.19
        Dextrose  .............  31.28
        Maltose  .............   7.31
        Sucrose  .............   1.31
        Higher Sugars  ........   1.50
Total Sugars ........................ 79.59%
Acids ............................  0.57%
Proteins ..........................  0.26%
Ash (minerals including iron, copper,
   potassium, sodium, phosphorus, mag-
   nesium, sulfur and silicon) ..........  0.17%
Minor components (including vitamins,
   pigments, flavorings and enzymes).... 2.21%
Water ............................ 17.20%
Total............................100.00%
```

A visit to the doctor, from folk artist Lewis Miller's sketchbook, about 1800.

The two major components of honey—levulose and
dextrose—are simple sugars. One argument made in favor
of eating honey is that these simple sugars are more easily
digestible than complex sugars. Our bodies must break
down complex sugars—such as sucrose, which is our ordinary table sugar—in order to make use of the energy they
contain. The sugars in honey are absorbed into the blood-
stream almost immediately.

Ever since the days of the ancient Greek Olympic
games, athletes have eaten honey as a source of quick
energy before attempting feats of strength or endurance.
Nor are athletes the only ones. The deep-sea diving crew
that helped salvage the ship Lusitania, sunk just before
World War I, was given a pound and a half of comb honey

Greek athletes. A detail from a Grecian vase.

for breakfast each morning. And later, during World War II, the British Royal Air Force pilots were given large amounts of honey as a restorative when they returned, exhausted, from their flying missions. Today, marathon runners, long distance swimmers, mountain climbers, and Arctic explorers all eat honey for energy.

As the chart shows, honey, unlike sugar, does contain measurable amounts of vitamins and minerals. But nutritionists don't agree on the value of these nutrients. Some think that the amounts are too small to be of any significance. Others think that even traces of certain minerals are valuable.

Recently, some research has suggested that it may be unwise to give honey to infants under one year of age. Studies done in California have raised the possibility that honey may be one of the sources through which very young infants are exposed to botulism. But, according to the Center for Disease Control, "the safety of honey as a food for older children and adults remains unquestioned."

Until a few hundred years ago, honey was the only concentrated sweet food available in most of the world. The Chinese sucked the sweet juice from sugar cane, and the Indians of North America boiled the sap of maple trees to make a thick syrup. But, except for honey, most people rarely tasted sweeteners. Their widespread use came only with the growth of the sugar industry in the seventeenth century, when sugar plantations were cultivated in the West Indies. Refined sugar was easier to ship, store, and use than honey—and it quickly became more popular.

Most people in the United States today choose sugar as their favorite sweetener. Each year, each American eats an average of one hundred pounds of sugar—and only two pounds of honey. Recently, however, many people have been turning back to honey because it is a more natural food.

Whatever the special advantages of honey, beekeepers have had the reputation of living to a very old age. If that is true, getting stung may be as responsible as eating honey— at least it has been claimed that bee venom is effective against rheumatism. The Essenes, an ancient Jewish tribe, were beekeepers famous for their longevity—most were said to live for more than one hundred years.

But the record may belong to an English beekeeper named Thomas Paar. He is said to have lived a quiet life in the countryside, drunk lots of honey wine, and eaten little, thus surviving to the age of 152. Then, in the year 1635, this remarkable man came to the attention of King Charles I, who invited him to a feast in London to honor his great age. There he ate too much and died.

The Tower of London.

BEDTIME MILK AND HONEY

Served hot at bedtime, an old-fashioned remedy for sleep-lessness.

1 cup milk   1 teaspoon honey

Warm the milk. Stir in 1 teaspoon of honey, and serve.

1 serving.

HOT LEMON AND HONEY

An old folk remedy to soothe sore throats, coughs, and colds.

1 cup hot water   *1 teaspoon honey*
1 teaspoon lemon juice   *3 cloves*

Pour hot water over the lemon juice, honey, and cloves. Steep 3 minutes. Remove cloves, stir, and serve.   *1 serving.*

CHAPTER THREE

In the Hive

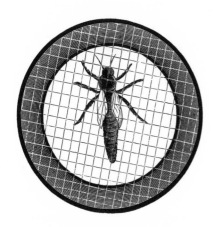

How doth the little busy bee
Improve each shining hour,
And gather honey all the day
From every opening flower.

How skillfully she builds her cell!
How neat she spreads the wax!
And labors hard to store it well
With the sweet food she makes!
—Isaac Watt

THE PROCESS by which bees make honey is one of the greatest marvels of nature. And yet it is only part of a still greater marvel—the complex system of behavior by which bees live, divide up their many duties, feed and defend themselves, communicate information, reproduce their species, adapt their lives to the changing seasons, and generally act for the good of the whole community instead of their individual selves. What makes this behavior all the more remarkable is that it is entirely instinctive—the bee carries it out automatically.

How bees reproduce their species wasn't understood until comparatively modern times. The most popular explanation was that bees arose from decaying meat, by "spontaneous generation." This idea came from a confusion of bees with flies. Flies aren't produced by spontaneous generation either, but they do sometimes lay their eggs in an animal carcass. Not observing the flies' tiny eggs, people assumed that the rotten flesh itself could somehow produce adult flies—and bees.

Inspired by this false belief, the ancients devised a special system for obtaining bees from a dead ox. The ox was beaten to death in a closed shed, which was then sealed shut and left for a long time. When the shed was opened at last, it was supposed to be full of bees! Needless to say, this method never worked.

Virgil, a Roman poet, who was deeply interested in bees—his father had been a beekeeper—advanced another theory, a more pleasant one, though no more accurate. It was his notion that bees simply gather their young from the sweet plants they visit.

This old print illustrates Virgil's notion of a "bee paradise."

Actually, the life cycle of the bee is complex and fascinating. The three kinds of bees in a beehive—drones, queen, and workers—are present in very unequal numbers. A typical hive may contain 200 drones, one queen, and 50,000 workers. These three types fulfill entirely different functions in the life of the hive.

The drones are the male bees. They have no part in making honey—in fact, their mouths are so designed that the job is impossible for them. They can't help to defend the hive because they have no stings. Their only role is to mate with newly-hatched queen bees.

This mating always takes place in mid-air. Each new queen soars away on what is called her "nuptial flight," and the fastest, strongest drones catch and mate with her. In the act of mating, their organs are ripped from their bodies and the drones die and fall to earth.

The queen bee, like the drone, has nothing to do with the making of honey. She has only one function in the hive—egg-laying. After mating, she begins laying the eggs—as many as 1500 a day, adding up to more than her own weight—from which young bees develop. Because queen bees live a few years and other bees live only a few weeks or months, it will not be long before she is the mother of every other bee in the hive.

If the hive needs to raise a new queen—for instance, if the old queen is gradually losing her egg-laying powers— the workers will produce a new queen from a worker egg. They do this by feeding royal jelly, a special food, to the immature insect—called a larva—that develops from the egg. How royal jelly works is not completely understood. But because it has the power to make a larva develop into a

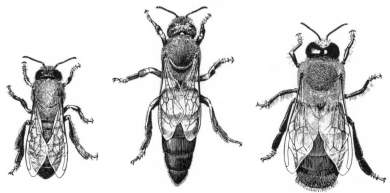

A worker, a queen, and a drone bee.

queen instead of just another worker, it is sometimes regarded as a miracle product. It can be obtained only in very small quantities; its chief commercial use is in beauty creams.

The queen bee requires continuous care. Her senses of sight, touch, and smell are poor, and she must be fed by the workers. They attend her constantly, licking and grooming her. As they do so, they detect a special substance, called simply "queen substance," that she secretes. This substance is passed from bee to bee, and acts to reassure them that the queen is still among them. If the queen is removed, every bee in the hive soon senses, from the disappearance of queen substance, that she is gone—a potentially disastrous event for the survival of the hive. At this point the bees will become disoriented and behave confusedly, especially if they are not well along toward raising a new queen for themselves.

The drones and the queen are responsible for reproduction—and nothing else. All of the remaining work of the hive is done by the workers. These are the proverbial "busy bees." They clean the hive, they guard it, they repair it, and—in the heat of summer—they fan their wings to cool it. They build honeycomb—sheets of six-sided cells—from beeswax, which they produce from glands on their abdomens. They care for the queen and they also take care of the young. Finally, they visit flowers, gathering the nectar and pollen that the hive requires for food.

The worker bee works herself to death. Her wings become so torn and tattered that she can no longer fly. But even in dying, her instincts direct her to help the community. She will probably die in the field. And if her final weakness overtakes her when she is within the hive, she will pull herself to the entrance and crawl away, which spares her sisters the task of removing her body.

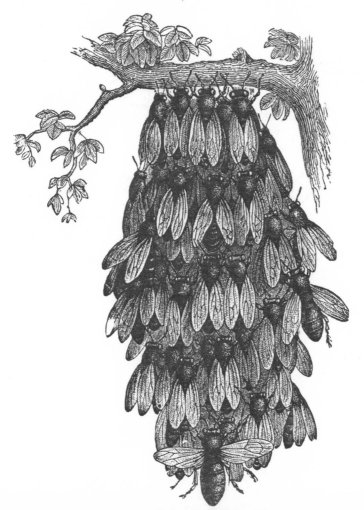

CHAPTER FOUR

How Do Bees Make Honey?

While honey lies in Every Flower, no doubt,
It takes a Bee to get the Honey out.
—Old Proverb

BEFORE it was understood how bees transform the nectar of flowers into honey, people assumed that honey just fell from the sky and that bees collected it from the blossoms where it landed.

The true explanation is far more interesting. A worker bee collects nectar by sucking it up from flowers with her long, seven-pronged tongue, one drop at a time. She stores it in a special part of her body, called a nectar sac. She goes from flower to flower until her nectar sac is full, and then she heads back toward the hive.

While the nectar is in her sac, it becomes more concentrated and some impurities are removed. Already, the honey-making has begun.

Back at the hive, the worker bee—called a "field bee" because she works outdoors—transfers her load of nectar to another worker bee whose duties are within the hive—a "house bee." Then the field bee returns to the fields to gather more nectar.

The house bee takes the nectar into her own nectar sac. She then opens her mouth and a drop of the nectar appears on her tongue. She passes the drop to another house bee. This process is repeated over and over. Water evaporates as the nectar is passed back and forth, making it thicker and more concentrated. The house bees add a substance called invertase, which also helps convert the nectar into honey.

After they have worked on the nectar for fifteen or twenty minutes, one of the house bees puts it into a cell of honeycomb. The comb looks fragile—its walls are only 1/500th of an inch thick—but it is strong; one pound of it will support twenty-five pounds of honey.

Nectar is sixty per cent water, and more than two-thirds of that water must evaporate for the nectar to thicken into honey. So the house bees fan it vigorously with their wings. Then the sweet fluid is left to thicken and ripen in the warm, dry air of the hive. When at last it reaches the right thickness, a house bee seals the cell with a cap of beeswax. It is now part of the food supply that will see the bees through the winter.

Bees are far more likely to visit some flowers than others. Because bees prefer sweet tastes—which they can detect not only with their mouths, but also with their antennae and their feet—they favor those flowers with the sweetest nectar.

The color of the flower, too, is important. The four main colors that bees can see are yellow, blue-green, blue, and ultra-violet (a color that humans can't see at all). Bees are chiefly attracted to flowers whose colors they can see.

When a field bee discovers a good source of nectar or pollen, she doesn't keep the information to herself. Bees tell each other about such finds with a most unusual form of communication: dancing.

The pattern and speed of the field bee's dance indicate how large her find is, which direction it's in, and how far

FROM THE 14th CENTURY LUTTRELL PSALTER

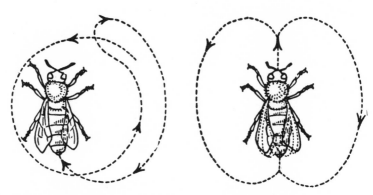

Bees perform the round dance (right) and the tail wagging dance (left) to give other bees information about the nectar sources they have found.

away it is. The other bees watch the dancer carefully and sometimes touch her, probably learning by taste and smell other information about what she has found.

There are two types of dances, the "round" dance and the "waggle-tail." The first is used to indicate nearby finds; the second is for more distant ones. After watching the dancer, some bees may fly off to her discovery while she is still dancing, and upon their return some of them may dance too. But their dance will be slower, indicating that the newly-discovered source has already been partly used up.

On each trip, a worker bee can bring home a load of nectar equal to her own weight. And yet all the nectar she collects in her lifetime will make only about one teaspoonful of honey.

CHAPTER FIVE

Other Honey-Makers

The Honey is sweet, but the Bee has a Sting.
—Benjamin Franklin,
Poor Richard's Almanack (1758)

O UR FAMILIAR honeybee isn't the only bee that makes honey. To begin with, she has three honeybee cousins that live in Asia. These are commonly called the Giant Bee, the Little Bee, and the Indian Bee.

Giant Bees are much larger than our domestic bee— they build an enormous sheet of honeycomb, up to six feet wide and two feet long. The Little Bee, by contrast, is about half the size of our honey bee. Its comb is just a few inches long and holds only a few ounces of honey.

Giant Bees and Little Bees cannot be kept commercially. They are too migratory—the whole colony will simply fly away if it takes a dislike to its living conditions. But occasionally people hunt for their wild nests and plunder them.

Indian Bees are more adaptable. They will sometimes nest in special indentations that farmers make in the outside walls of their houses. But, like Little Bees, they produce only a small amount of honey.

[35]

The familiar bumblebee may look something like an oversized honeybee, but it differs sharply from the honeybee in its cycle of life. Among bumblebees, only the queen lives through the winter. In the spring, she looks for the abandoned nest of a mouse or other small animal in which to lay her eggs. Or she will nest in a clump of dried grass, if that is all she can find. She leaves her nest only to go foraging for nectar and pollen.

Soon after she has eaten this food, her body begins to produce wax, which she uses to build a small pot inside the entrance to the nest, and a small wax cell. The bumblebee queen fills the pot with nectar, and the cell with pollen. Then she lays her eggs in the cell and sits on them, the way a chicken does. The nectar and pollen she has stored serve as her food during bad weather. And they will also be food for the first crop of baby bumblebees that hatch.

Since bumblebees (except for the queen) do not survive the winter, they have no need to build up a surplus of food. So they never produce enough honey to be of commercial value. Honeybees, by contrast, do survive the winter, huddling into a ball for warmth and eating their stored supply of honey.

Another honey-producing bee is the stingless bee of South America, Asia, and Australia. Although these bees are stingless, they are far from defenseless. They attack invading humans, biting them, secreting a burning fluid on their skins, and swarming into their noses, eyes, and ears. Nevertheless, the Mayans of South America learned long ago to keep stingless bees in hollow logs and collect from them a thin sweet honey. Yields, however, tend to be low. Whereas bumblebees store no excess honey because they don't live through the winter, stingless bees store little surplus because, in the tropical regions where the Mayans live, there *is* no winter. With flowers available the year round, stingless bees never need to accumulate much more honey than they can eat in a day.

Mayan figures: two bees on either side of a mead jar.

A kind of honey is also produced by certain wasps, found in South America. Most wasps lead solitary lives, but these honey-making wasps live in colonies as bees do. Scientists aren't sure just what the wasps use their honey for. It is probably stored, mostly as a reserve food, to be eaten by the colony in times of drought. Though the baby wasps are occasionally given honey, they are usually fed meat.

And then there is honeydew, a sweet, sticky, honey-like fluid that is secreted by aphids. These tiny greenish creatures infest plants and trees, sucking out sap. After extracting the proteins and minerals they need, the aphids expel the remainder of the fluid, which, in the process of passing through them, has become honeydew.

Honeydew sometimes appears in enormous quantities. The leaves of trees may be shiny with it, and it may be so abundant that it drops to the ground like misty rain. The

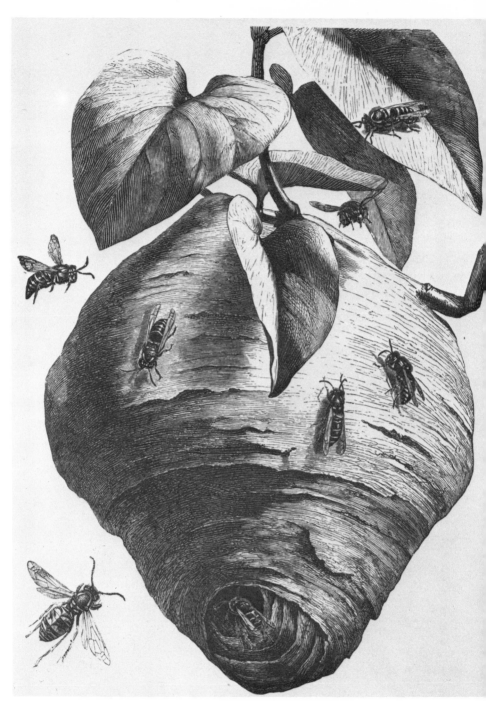

A wasp's nest.

Bible tells of "manna from Heaven" that fell from the skies and kept the Hebrews from starving during their desert wanderings. Some people believe that this miracle was actually a honeydew shower.

When fresh, honeydew is clear in color and has such a pleasant flavor that bees will collect it. But the honey they produce from honeydew is usually of inferior quality.

Aphids, the tiny insects that produce honeydew, are not kept by man. Amazingly enough, however, aphids are kept by certain kinds of ants. These ants love the sweet honeydew, eat it, and even store it away, using a system of storage that is all their own.

Ants collect honeydew either from the ground where it has fallen or by actually "milking" the aphids. To milk an aphid, an ant taps it on the hind end until a drop appears on the tip of the aphid's abdomen. Then the ant sucks up the drop.

Ants and aphids interact in a variety of ways. Some merely take fluid from aphids whenever they happen to come across them. Other ants collect aphids and build earth walls around them. Or they dig pits for their aphids at the base of plants. The aphids live in the pits and swarm up the plants to get food. Sometimes ants keep aphid eggs underground in their ant nests, during the winter. In the spring they carry the newborn aphids out of the nests and put them on roots to feed.

Though it may seem at first as though the aphids are the ants' slaves, actually both species benefit by living together. The aphids are protected from predators, and the ants obtain food.

Ants don't store the fluid they collect in cells, the way

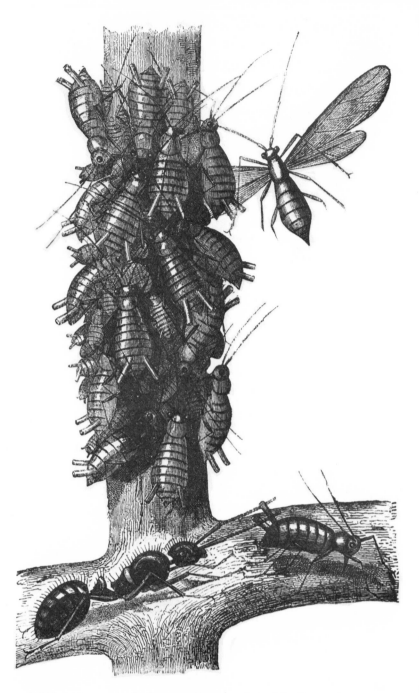

Aphids and ants. In the foreground, an ant is "milking" an aphid.

bees do. Instead, they store it in other ants. These storage ants are called repletes, or honeypots. Ants bringing honeydew back to the ant nest regurgitate it into the honeypots.

As these honeypots become fuller and fuller, they grow enormously round. They crawl to the roof of the ant nest and hang there. Other ants crawl up and continue to feed them. Eventually the honeypots look like fat yellow balls. They can hold up to eight times their own weight in honey.

Like the honeycombs of bees, honeypot ants serve as a kind of community savings account. During rainy seasons, when the aphids are producing well, the honeypots are filled up. In dry weather, when nourishment is scarce, they pass the contents back to other ants for food.

Honeypot ants are a prized delicacy among the aborigines of Australia and some native tribes of South America, who dig up the ant nests and pull out the swollen honeypots. They either eat the whole honeypot or just bite off its huge yellow abdomen to enjoy a mouthful of sweetness.

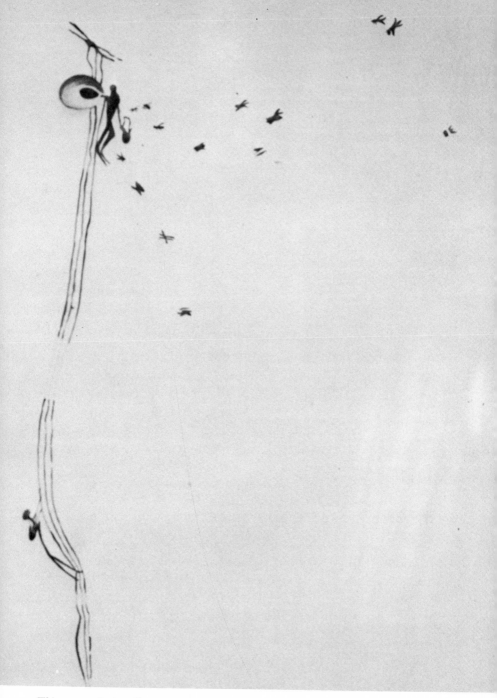

This cave painting discovered in Bicorp, Spain, is the earliest known record of honey hunting

CHAPTER SIX

Honey Hunters

> *It is not with saying Honey, Honey, that
> sweetness comes into the mouth.*
> —Turkish proverb

HONEY was the richest and most delicious substance that early people ever tasted. Most other foods that they gathered or hunted, and devoured half-raw, were bland and tough. But honey was smooth, thick, and wonderfully sweet. Once people had tasted it they longed to have it again. They risked painful bee stings and sometimes even death to get at this fabulous food.

The first honey came from the nests of wild bees. A cave painting at Araña, Spain, shows two men trying to reach a bees' nest high on a cliff. The men are climbing a long hanging ladder, probably woven of grass, and carrying skin bags to put the honey into. They are naked and completely unprotected against stings as they sway on the fragile ladder. This painting is about fifteen thousand years old.

At first, early people gathered honey only when they were lucky enough to come across a wild nest. But then they realized that the discovery of beehives did not need to be left to chance. Watch a bee closely, sometime, as she moves from flower to flower. When she is fully loaded with nectar or pollen, she will head back toward her hive in a

Determined honey hunters off on a chase.

line so straight that it gives us the proverbial expression for a direct route—a "beeline."

Since bees fly at an average speed of fifteen miles per hour, you probably won't be able to keep up with her, but at least you will know in which direction to look. With persistence, you may be able to find her hive. Using the same technique, the early honey hunters found many a wild hive in a hollow tree or under a rock.

In colonial America, professional honey hunters ranged through the wilderness. When they located a wild nest in a hollow tree they chopped down the tree with an ax and collected the honeycombs in buckets. Then they headed for the nearest settlement to exchange the honey for food and supplies. The lives of colonial honey hunters were lonely and dangerous, but there was always a demand for their product because sugar was scarce and expensive well into the eighteenth century.

Even today some honey hunters take great risks in order to get honey. In India, tribesmen climb dangerously steep rock faces to get at the combs of the Giant Bee. If they slip, they may be smashed to death on the rocks below. And they risk getting hundreds of stings from these fierce bees, who are so aggressive that they will rush out of their nests after an intruder, stinging him again and again as he flees. Even diving into water does not bring safety; the bees wait for their victim to surface and attack him again.

Honey hunting is a ritual for many tribes. The Mbuti Pygmies, who live in the Ituri forest of Zaire, hunt in families, searching carefully through the trees. When they locate a nest, usually in a hollow tree, the father of the family climbs the tree carrying a burning, smoky stick. He pushes the stick into the hive to drive out the bees. Then he reaches in, ignoring any stings he receives in the process,

The German Zeidler (forest beekeeper) carried a crossbow to discourage hunters from pillaging nests in his woodlands.

pulls out the honeycombs, and throws them down to the women and children below. They pack the combs into woven baskets and carry them home.

The Onges, who live in the Adaman Islands off the coast of India, also hunt honey in family groups. But they have a better way of dealing with the bees. When a nest is discovered, the father of the family chews the leaves of a special plant. He smears the pulp on his body before climbing the tree. The bees seem to be repelled by this substance and will not sting him. As he climbs, he spits out bits of the pulp at the hovering bees.

Among both the Mbuti Pygmies and the Onges, stealing another family's honey is punished by banishment from the tribe. In the desolate areas where these peoples live, banishment nearly always results in death. Yet occasionally tribespeople have such a passionate desire for honey that they risk this horrible fate.

Other honey hunters are sometimes helped by an amazing bird called the honey guide, which lives in Africa and Southern Asia. It is just what its name implies—a bird that guides people to honey.

The honey guide approaches someone and perches on a nearby branch, making a churring noise and fanning its tail to attract attention. When the person comes near, the bird flies to another tree and waits there, signaling again. This pattern continues until the honey guide has led the way to a bees' nest. The distance covered may be as great as a mile.

As the person removes the honey, the honey guide watches from a tree branch. Afterward, the bird swoops down and eats bits of wax comb that have been left lying about. For the honey guide is a real rarity—one of the very few creatures that can digest wax.

The bird's problem, of course, is getting the wax out of the bees' nest. Since it can't do this itself, it has evolved instinctive behavior for leading a honey-loving creature—like man—to open the nest and expose the wax. But in fact the creature does not have to be human—any honey-loving animal able to open a bees' nest will do. Honey guides sometimes lead badgers to nests, and sometimes baboons. They have been seen trying to lead monkeys and mongooses, but these creatures will rarely follow them.

Badgers and baboons react to the honey guide instinctively, just as it does to them. But human beings' responses to the bird have been more thoughtful. Some have tried to attract it by imitating the grunting of a badger, or by pounding on trees to suggest the sound of a beehive being opened.

Honey guides often lead honey badgers to wild bees' nests.

There are many stories and folk tales about this remarkable bird. One Rhodesian myth says that a long time ago a honey guide came upon a dead elephant. He was happy at finding so much food and decided to call his friends and relatives to share in the feast. He made a mark on the elephant's body to identify it as his own. Then he went off.

While he was gone, a mouse found the elephant and began to eat it. When the bird returned, he was angry. "This is mine," he said. "No," said the mouse, "it's mine." They argued and finally went to see the judge, who was a honeybee. He said to the bird, "You are lying. The elephant belongs to the mouse."

Since that day, honey guides and bees have been enemies. And that, according to the myth, is why the honey guide leads people and animals to the bees' nests.

CHAPTER SEVEN

The First Beekeepers

He who with health would live at ease,
Should cultivate both fruit and bees.
—English proverb

THE HONEY we eat comes from domesticated honeybees. We call them that because they live in our man-made hives, not in nests they have built themselves.

But honeybees live according to their age-old instincts. We can never domesticate them in the sense that we can dogs or horses—animals that can be trained. The story of our "domestication" of bees is the story of our slow education in how they work. Gradually we have learned to arrange their living conditions so that they can produce more honey than they themselves need to eat. This makes it possible for the beekeeper to take the extra honey to eat or sell without depriving the bees of their food.

The first step toward real beekeeping came when early people began marking certain trees to claim ownership of the hives in them. The next stage, and a crucial one, was somehow getting the beehive home. Stone Age people chipped away sections of hollow logs that contained bee-

dye deu neft Weet dyen Deeten
dyen Roft du heeten

The Beekeepers, by Peter Bruegal, 1565.

hives and carried them off. Now the hives were conveniently close at hand.

Soon people began to make hives for the bees to live in. Sometimes they used a section of hollowed-out log, or a clay jug with a narrow spout. Other hives, called "skeps," were built up from coils of straw.

But once the hives were constructed, how did you get the bees to live in them? People learned to rub the insides of the new hives with sweet-smelling herbs like rosemary and thyme, and to smear them with a little honey. And they discovered that bees could be pacified with smoke, making it possible to move them from a wild nest to a man-made hive with much less likelihood of being stung.

They also discovered that it was not very dangerous to capture a swarm—a large number of bees that have left their hive, usually because of overcrowding, and settled down in a clinging mass, often hanging from the limb of a tree. Bees in a swarm are unlikely to sting. They can simply be swept into a container and taken home. Since they are looking for a new home anyway, the beekeeper may well be able to persuade them to accept his hospitality.

After all, by the bees' standards, even primitive hives made good homes. They had narrow openings which the bees could defend. They offered protection against extreme heat and cold, against wind and rain. Wood and clay hives were naturally waterproof; straw ones were made waterproof with smearings of mud and dung.

With the rise of civilization generally, beekeeping around the world developed in different ways, depending on local circumstances. For instance, the ancient Egyptians sometimes sent hives to the southern part of their country

This bas-relief from an Egyptian temple shows beekeepers of 2600 B.C. tending their hives.

for the beginning of the beekeeping season, because plants flowered earlier there. Then the hives were placed on rafts and floated slowly north on the Nile, keeping pace with the advancing season, so the bees would always have newly-opened flowers to draw nectar from. At the end of the season, the honey-rich hives arrived in Cairo, and the honey was harvested and sold. Honey was so valued that the Egyptian hieroglyph for "bee" became a symbol of the Pharaohs.

As beekeeping became a profitable enterprise, inevitably it fell under the control of law. The Hittite Code, about 300 B.C., even set the value of honey—a tub of it was worth the same as a tub of butter or one sheep.

The lore of beekeeping developed, too—part science, but mostly superstition. For example, the Jewish Talmud warned beekeepers not to let mustard plants grow near the hive, because the bees would burn their throats on the mustard blossoms. Then they would eat honey to cool off, leaving less for the beekeeper. An old Arabic medical work suggested that, in order to keep away wax moths (whose larvae ruin honeycomb), fresh milk and the urine of children should be sprinkled over the legs of the hive.

One especially persistent myth is that bees can be summoned with loud noises. Even into our own century, many people have believed that they could attract bees by whistling or ringing a bell. Actually, bees have poor hearing and cannot be attracted by sounds.

Another common myth was that bees must be told anything important that happened in their owner's household—a birth, a death, a wedding. On happy occasions, bright ribbons were attached to the hives; during funerals, pieces of black crepe. If the bees weren't properly informed, it was thought, they would refuse to produce honey. An Irish ditty says:

> *A maiden in her glory,*
> *Upon her wedding day,*
> *Must tell the bees her story,*
> *Or else they'll fly away.*

Although such great care was taken of the bees' feelings, collecting their honey was always an act of destruction. It meant driving the bees from the hive, or more often, killing the entire colony. This was the trouble with most early hives. What beekeepers needed was a way to remove the honeycomb without sacrificing the bees, ruining the comb, or damaging the hive. Unless and until such a hive could be developed, the science of beekeeping could never progress much beyond its primitive beginnings.

CHAPTER EIGHT

Money from Honey: Modern Beekeeping

*If you want to gather honey,
don't kick over the beehive.*
—Abraham Lincoln

HOW DO MODERN beehives help the beekeeper—and the bee? There are two basic principles in their design. One has been known since the early days of beekeeping, but the other was discovered only in the last century.

The first principle is that individual sections of comb must be removable separately, leaving the hive undamaged, and disturbing the bees as little as possible. Ancient Greek hives were woven baskets with the open end on top. This end was covered with wooden bars, from which the bees hung their combs. When the bars were lifted, the combs could be removed. Unfortunately, this practical design seems to have been unknown outside of Greece until the end of the Middle Ages.

Many attempts were made to improve on this hive during the seventeenth and eighteenth centuries. One important step was to give the bees not just single bars lying across the top of the hive, but complete four-sided frames that could be removed from the hive. The idea was that the

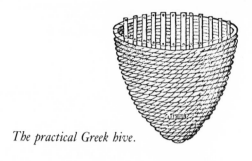

The practical Greek hive.

bees would construct their honeycomb in neat rectangular sections within the frames, which could then be lifted out of the hive.

The trouble was that the bees kept fastening the frames to the sides of the hive. And it was not until 1851 that this persistent problem was solved. In that year, an American beekeeper, the Reverend Lorenzo Langstroth, discovered the second essential principle of the modern hive—the principle of the "bee space." The bee space is a passageway, three-eighths of an inch wide, between the edge of the frame and the side of the hive. Bees will use a space precisely this wide, Langstroth discovered, to crawl about within the hive. If the space is wider, the bees will instinctively fill it up with honeycomb, which will be torn when the frame is lifted out, thereby wasting precious honey. On the other hand, if the space is *narrower* than three-eighths of an inch, the bees will cement the frame to the hive with propolis, a sticky sealant that they make from tree sap.

Langstroth's discovery of the bee space led to the development of the modern hive. It consists of a series of boxes stacked one on top of another. Nine or ten rectangular frames, in which the bees build honeycomb, hang within each box. One box, usually the bottom one, is reserved for the queen's egg-laying. The queen is confined to this box by a mesh frame—called a queen excluder—laid on top of it. It prevents her from laying eggs in the upper boxes, which the beekeeper wants to reserve for honey storage. The holes in the mesh are big enough for the worker bees to pass through, but too small for the queen. More honey storage boxes are added on top as necessary to keep up with the hive's production.

At first the bees built their honeycombs directly on the bare wood frame. Then beekeepers found that wax sheets, stamped with the outlines of honeycomb, could be produced by machine and fitted into standard-sized frames.

A modern hive, cut away to show the movable frames inside.

Using this foundation as a base, the bees can build their honeycomb much more quickly. This leaves them more time for making honey.

After honey is gathered from the hives, it can be eaten right in the comb. Usually, however, it is packaged for sale in liquid form. The first liquid honey was made by crushing and straining full honeycombs, but the honey was never very clear. It included particles of crushed pollen, wax, propolis, and bits of bees.

Then, in the 1860's, an Austrian, Major Francis Hruschka, invented an extractor that used centrifugal force to separate the honey from the comb. It's said that Hruschka got the idea for his invention when he saw a little boy who was holding a basket of uncapped honeycombs suddenly raise the basket and swing it about his head. The liquid honey flew out but the combs stayed in the basket.

The extractor works on the same principle. First, the wax caps are sliced off the honeycomb. Then the uncapped combs are placed in the extractor, which whirls them around until the honey is thrown out of the cells.

Extraction usually takes place in a special building called a honey house. After the liquid honey is removed from the comb, it is strained. Then the honey is pumped to settling tanks where it stays for a day or two. During this time, fine particles that the straining didn't remove settle to the bottom. Air bubbles that have been caused by all the handling disappear. If the bubbles were allowed to remain they would give the honey a cloudy appearance. Sometimes the honey is also heated to prevent it from granulating or fermenting. Finally, the honey is bottled.

Modern beekeeping is practiced on every scale from a

A beekeeper placing frames of honeycomb in his extractor.

single hive in the back yard to huge bee farms with thousands of hives. It can be a satisfying hobby or a profitable business. But science hasn't yet solved all the beekeeper's problems.

Honeybees are subject to a number of serious diseases. Extremes of weather are a threat to them, too. It is almost never too hot for bees, but it is often too cold, too wet, or too dry. A bad summer can cut back honey production drastically and a hard winter can kill every bee in the hive.

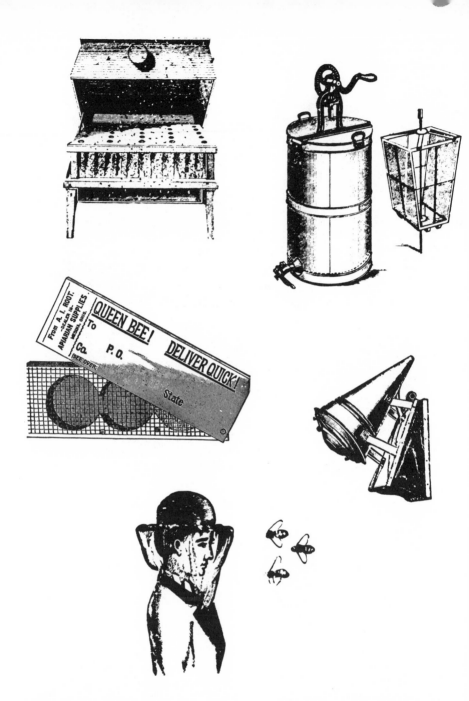

In the second half of the 19th century, all sorts of beekeeping devices were marketed (clockwise from top left): new hives, extractors, smokers to pacify the bees, bee veils to protect against stings, special boxes to ship queen bees from keeper to keeper.

Man isn't the only animal that loves honey, so beekeepers have to be prepared for unwanted visitors. The
largest animals likely to come calling are bears. Bears' love
of honey is so well-known that it has become legendary.
They will destroy every hive they can find, and lick up not
only the honey but also the larvae and even the adult bees.
Of course, bears live mostly in wilderness areas today. In
the few spots where they remain a problem to beekeepers,
hives are often protected by wire fences charged with a
mild electric current—just enough to frighten the bears
away.

These days, skunks are more likely to trouble the beekeeper than bears are. They're actually more interested in
eating the bees than the honey. Skunks come and scratch at
the hives at night, then gobble up the bees when they come
out to investigate.

An even more common nuisance is mice. They are
small enough to enter hives through the narrow slot that the
bees themselves use. Once inside, they love to chew the
honeycomb. Bees will often sting an invading mouse to
death, but this presents them with a new problem: what to
do with the mouse's body, which is too heavy for them to
haul out. If it is simply left there, it will decompose and
contaminate the hive. So the bees seal it up with propolis,
the special glue that they make. This preserves it by keeping out air-borne bacteria.

It is other insects, however, that are bees' most dangerous enemies—and the greatest hazard to the beekeeper.
Bees sometimes suffer the invasions of ants, and fatal infes-
tations of lice. Among flying insects, bees' greatest enemies

are wax moths, whose larvae tunnel through and ruin the honeycomb.

And beekeepers have to guard against a very odd phenomenon. If honeybees are ever permitted to get into honey that they haven't made themselves, there is a great risk that they will stop gathering nectar and become robber bees.

Ordinarily, bees are not interested in stealing honey—especially when the flowers are producing a lot of nectar. But when the weather is bad and the flowers are fading, bees sometimes take to robbing.

At times, robber bees gather together in large numbers. They smash their way into other hives, and fight with and often destroy the defending bees. Sometimes the defeated bees join the victors for the next invasion. So beekeepers try not to give robbing a chance to start. They don't leave honeycomb or extracted honey lying around. They make sure the honey house is bee-proof. And they take good care of their bees so that colonies will be healthy and strong enough to fight off invaders.

Although honey production is an important industry in the United States, honeybees are not native to North America. They were brought here by the early colonists. It is not known exactly when the first shipment of bees arrived. But records show that a bee farm was established in the town of Newbury, Massachusetts, in 1640. It is also recorded that the first beekeeper lost all his money and became Newbury's first pauper.

Obviously, the time for commercial beekeeping had not yet arrived. But honeybees soon came to flourish in America—and were highly valued. In 1641, bee colonies in New England were selling for five pounds apiece. This price was equivalent to the wages a skilled craftsman received for fifteen days of work.

As the settlers advanced westward across North America, they brought honeybees with them. The Indians had never seen these insects. They called them "English flies" or "white man's flies," and dreaded their appearance because it meant the arrival of new settlers. In the poem "Hiawatha," written by Henry Wadsworth Longfellow in 1855, an Indian speaker says,

> *"Wheresoe'er they move, before them*
> *Swarms the stinging fly, the Ahmo,*
> *Swarms the Bee, the honey-maker."*

Honeybees were first brought to the west coast of North America by boat, around the middle of the nineteenth century. In that mild climate, where flowers and shrubs flourished, so did bees. Today bees are kept, sometimes for profit and sometimes for pleasure, in every state of the union.

CHAPTER NINE

Useful Honey

Sugar in the gourd and honey in the horn.
I never was so happy since the hour I was born.
—"Turkey in the Straw"

A FOOD, a drink, a beauty treatment. A magical substance, a sacred offering. A flytrap, a weapon, a form of money. The last bath of dead kings.

Down through the ages, honey has been all these things and more. Today, ninety per cent of all honey harvested is used as a pure table food—poured onto pancakes and waffles, stirred into drinks as a sweetener, spread on toast, or used as a topping for desserts.

Honey is included in prepared foods as well, not just for its taste, but also for its moisture-preserving quality. Commercial bakers use honey to make their cakes and breads moist and long-lasting.

Other modern uses of honey may surprise you. It is an important ingredient in chewing gum and in making sticky sprays. It is used as a coating to help preserve the flavor of coffee beans. It is sometimes added to livestock feed. It helps attract houseflies to their final roosts on strips of fly paper. Honey ages and sweetens pipe bowls and, because of its low freezing point, it is used as anti-freeze in cars.

Since prehistoric times, honey has been used to make alcoholic beverages. Mead—the age-old honey wine—has been almost entirely displaced by wine made from grapes. But honey is now an ingredient in several liquors. Athol Brose, a famous Scottish liquor, is made with honey, rich cream, and Scotch whiskey. Another liquor called Drambuie contains honey, whiskey, and special spices.

Perhaps just as old as the drinking of honey is its use in cosmetics. Poppea, the wife of the Roman emperor Nero, is said to have used a face lotion made from honey and asses'

milk. In the eighteenth century, Queen Anne of England frequently treated her hair with a warm solution of honey and oil. The use of honey as a cosmetic face mask was widely recommended. One old formula for erasing "skin discoloration," which probably meant freckles, called for daily applications of honey and watercress juice.

In our own time, honey is again becoming an important and popular ingredient in cosmetics. Many people prefer to avoid creams and lotions that contain synthetic chemicals. So, more and more, they are making their own preparations from natural ingredients. Honey retards the growth of bacteria and helps the skin retain moisture. It is fragrant and mixes easily with many other natural substances. Some recipes for honey cosmetics are given at the end of this chapter.

Because it was universally desired, widely available, and more or less standard in quality, honey was sometimes used in the ancient world as a medium of exchange, a form of money. In the Roman empire, citizens often paid their taxes with honey. And the Romans would accept honey in payment of tribute from conquered nations. Honey could be used to buy other foods, household furnishings, even farm animals. The amount of honey a person owned was one measure of his wealth.

Another use of honey belonging entirely to the past was as a preservative for dead bodies. Kings of Sparta had themselves embalmed in honey. So did Alexander the Great: as he had commanded, his body was laid in a golden coffin filled with white honey. The winding sheets that the ancient Egyptians used to mummify their Pharaohs were soaked in a mixture of honey and spices. This helped keep out destructive bacteria.

A medieval artist's idea of how bees might be used in warfare.

A still stranger, and certainly rarer, use of honey was in warfare. It is entertaining legend, not fact, that the Union Army used bees as carrier pigeons to smuggle tiny messages through Confederate lines during the Civil War. But the truth of older reports is harder to judge. According to ancient writers, hives of bees were sometimes hurled at enemy armies. And there is one report of poison honey being used. Vessels of this honey were placed in the path of the advancing army. When the enemy soldiers ate the honey they became ill and were easy to overpower.

This sounds like myth, but it may have happened. Today we do know of a few poisonous honeys. One is made from the nectar of the mountain laurel and others come from plants that grow in New Zealand. These honeys have been known to make people feel ill and even lose consciousness, though no one has died. Naturally, beekeepers don't locate their hives near these sources, but occasionally wild bees collect the nectar and produce the dangerous honey.

Honey has had many uses—some familiar, some strange. But it has often been regarded as much more than merely a practical substance. In the next chapter we shall look at this other history of honey—honey the mysterious, the magical, even the divine.

HONEY MASK

A relaxing treatment to tighten skin, close pores, and smooth lines. The egg white and honey make a watertight film that helps the skin accumulate moisture.

1 egg white
1 tablespoon honey
3 tablespoons barley flour

½ teaspoon orange flower water *
or rosewater (optional)

Whip the egg white until it forms soft peaks. Gently fold in the honey and barley flour. Add the orange flower water. Pat a thick layer of the mask on your face and leave it on for 15 minutes or longer. Wash it off with warm water. Then rinse with cool water. *1 treatment.*

*Orange flower water and rosewater may be purchased at specialty food stores, or cologne may be substituted.

HONEY PASTE FOR CHAPPED HANDS

An old English recipe for a home-made paste to smooth rough, chapped hands.

1 egg white   *1 teaspoon honey*
1 teaspoon glycerine *   *barley flour*

Mix the first three ingredients thoroughly. Then add just enough barley flour to form a smooth paste, about 4 tablespoons. This will keep 3 days in the refrigerator in a covered container. Rub a small amount into your hands as needed.   *4 treatments.*

HONEY LOTION

This is a very thin lotion used to soften the skin.

2 tablespoons honey   *⅛ teaspoon perfume (optional)*
2 tablespoons lemon juice

Mix all the ingredients thoroughly. Pat a small amount onto your hands or face and gently massage it into the skin. Store the rest in a covered container.   *4 treatments.*

*Glycerine is sold at most drugstores.

HONEY FACE CREAM

A fragrant, moisturizing face cream that will keep indefinitely.

½ cup beeswax *   *1 tablespoon sweet almond oil*
¾ cup honey   *perfume (optional)*

Put the beeswax in a container in a pan of hot water. Heat the water over a low flame until the wax melts. Stir in the honey and almond oil. Remove from the heat. Stir until the mixture cools. Add a few drops of your favorite perfume. Keep in a jar with a tightly fitting cover. Moisten your hands before applying the cream.

   * Beeswax may be purchased at most hobby stores.

ne uisunt cuncti. p̄ amiciciam sibi uincti. Huic conuiuiante̅ & eius a munera

opus ablatis tribus & septe̅ sibi natis. Iob recipit totideos meditsit qua̅ fuit

CHAPTER TEN

Divine Honey

Out of the eater came something to eat,
Out of the strong came something sweet.
—Judges 14:14

IT IS EASY to imagine why, of all the substances known to man, honey came to have special religious significance.

For one thing, the way bees make honey was not entirely understood. Honey could therefore be seen as a gift from heaven.

Another reason is simply that honey tastes so wonderfully good. Since the gods—it was assumed—could eat whatever they wanted, it seemed logical that they would choose honey, the most delicious food of all.

Honey was also important to religion because it was used to make mead, the earliest alcoholic beverage. When mixed with water, honey ferments quickly, and becomes intoxicating. Ancient people probably learned this accidentally by tasting water in which honeycombs had been lying. The strange sensations that followed mead-drinking may have seemed proof of its divine origin.

One of the most widespread uses of honey in religion was as a sacrifice to the gods. Sometimes the sacrificed honey was baked into cakes that were then either burned or simply left at a spot considered sacred. But more often the honey was poured out in liquid form—a style of offering known as a libation.

In many ancient religions it was believed that the gods lived on honey and that they might even lose their divinity if they couldn't get it. In fact, one widespread belief was that honey was originally a food *only* of the gods, and that men had stolen some from them. So, in several religions, the gods were said to post a guard over their honey. In Greek and Indian religion, it was an eagle; in Norse religion, it was the god Odin.

Sometimes the ancients used honey to confer holiness. Priests smeared themselves with honey before praying or performing rituals. They fed it to sacred animals. The ancient Babylonians dedicated their new buildings, and sought divine favor for them, by smearing honey on their thresholds.

Because of its supposedly divine nature, honey was thought to give people special powers, especially the power of eloquent speech. Perhaps it was the sweet taste of honey in the mouth that first suggested it could make a person an orator or poet. According to tradition, Homer, Sophocles, Plato, and Virgil all had their lips touched with honey in their infancies. And priestesses in ancient Greece were said to have gained the gift of prophecy from eating honey.

Honey was often given to newborn infants as a kind of initiation into the world. The ancient Egyptians, Babylonians, and Hebrews fed milk and honey to their children as their first food. That, it was considered, made the baby a real human being, with the rights and privileges of other members of his society.

In an age when nearly everyone's living depended on

Egyptian tomb drawings illustrated important scenes from daily life; this one from about 600 B.C. shows a man with honeybees and hives.

agriculture, honey was used as a magical charm to ensure good crops. According to the German custom called *Acker-segam*, if a farmer was worried about his crops, he poured a mixture of milk and honey into the first furrow in each field.

It was the Hindu religion, though, to which bees were most significant. The gods Vishnu and Krishna were called Mudhava, "the nectar-born ones." The bee was their symbol. Vishnu is usually represented as a blue bee resting on a flower. Krishna, resembling a young man, is portrayed with a blue bee on or above his forehead. Because the basil plant was sacred to these two gods, Hindus would hold some basil while taking honey from a beehive.

Part of every religion concerns death, and honey has
been associated with death in many ways. People who
believed in an afterlife, like the ancient Egyptians, often
took the practical measure of packing away some honey
with a dead person—especially if he had been rich and
powerful—so that he would have this most delicious of
foods at hand when he returned to life.

*The bee figured in many Egyptian hieroglyphs: on the left, the symbol for honey;
on the right, the symbol for death.*

In some ancient religions, like that of the Greeks, honey
served as a bridge between the worlds of the dead and the
living. People who wanted to summon up the spirits of
dead ancestors, or soothe spirits that they feared they had
offended, would make them an offering of honey.

In the Bible, honey suggests whatever is sweet and
desirable, from love to religious exaltation. Thus, the Song
of Songs has the passionate bridegroom saying, "Your lips
drop sweetness like the honeycomb, my bride," while the
Psalms of David say, "The judgement of the Lord is
sweeter than honey and the droppings of the honeycomb."
The description of Palestine as "a land flowing with milk
and honey" is meant, not, of course, as a literal description,
but as a phrase suggesting abundant prosperity.

An unusual nesting place for bees is described in the story of Samson, who killed a lion and later found a hive in its carcass. He removed the honey. As he did so, the peculiarity of its location suggested to him the riddle that appears below the title of this chapter.

Today, the Jewish religion still involves the eating of honey once a year at the traditional Passover feast. It is prepared in a mixture called *charoses,* which symbolizes the mortar that the ancient Hebrews used in building the pyramids when they were slaves in Egypt. You will find a recipe for *charoses* on page 126.

In the King James Bible, the most important mention of honey occurs after Christ's resurrection. The foods given him by his overjoyed disciples were fish and honey. "And while they believed not for joy, and wondered, He said

ROBINSONS BRISTOL

unto them, 'Have ye here any meat?' And they gave Him a
piece of broiled fish and of a honeycomb. He took it and did
eat before them" (Luke 24:41). This meal has not only nu-
tritional value but also a special spiritual value. As we have
seen, honey was a food traditionally associated with divinity, and a fish was a specifically Christian symbol.

In the Church of Jesus Christ of Latter-Day Saints,
often known as the Mormon religion, the honeybee symbolizes hard work. In 1849, Mormons proposed the forma-
tion of a huge state in the American west. It was to be
called "Deseret," which is the sacred word for "honeybee"
in the Book of Mormon. The great state of Deseret never
came to be, but today the official seal of the state of Utah,
where many Mormons live, has a beehive at its center.
Above is the word "Industry"—the trait for which bees are
legendary, and, for Mormons, one of the highest virtues.

CHAPTER ELEVEN

How to Buy Honey

The Pedigree of honey
Does not concern the bee;
A clover, any time, to him
Is aristocracy.
— Emily Dickinson

THE HONEY buyer has a dazzling choice of honeys from every part of the world. Honeys have very different tastes and appearances depending on the blossoms from which the bees have gathered their nectar. In the United States alone, one can choose among golden alfalfa honey, dark avocado honey, California orange blossom or sage honey, water-white huajillo honey from Texas, and hundreds of others.

Some honeys are mild; others taste strong, spicy, bitter-sweet, or herblike. In general, the darker honeys have stronger tastes, which some people—but not all—love. And darker honeys are said to have more mineral content. The light-colored honeys are usually mild in flavor and fragrance and are universally enjoyed.

Clover honey, the most widely used honey in the United States, is light amber in color, delicate and mellow in flavor. From the flowers of buckwheat, grown in the Northeastern states, bees make a dark, hearty honey.

Golden orange-blossom honey from California and Florida has the tantalizing taste and aroma of oranges. Tupelo honey, from the Southeastern United States, is prized by honey lovers for its rich, intoxicating sweetness.

Many delicious honeys are imported from abroad. Julius Caesar was said to love an extremely fragrant white rosemary honey, which is still available from the neighborhood of Narbonne, in France. During his campaigns against the Gauls, he reportedly had vessels of this delicious honey sent to him along with military dispatches.

Jasmine honey—from the same flowers that yield jasmine perfume—and sea-green gooseberry honey are other French specialties. Wild thyme honey—"the food of the gods"—from Mount Hymettus in Greece has a wonderful herb scent and flavor. Thick Scottish heather honey has a rich, candy-like taste and appearance. Every beekeeping region of the world boasts a special honey.

Many people believe that honey in the comb, just as it was sealed in by the bees, is the purest and tastiest kind. The most common way of eating it is to slice off a piece, put it in your mouth, and chew it. Your teeth will crush the delicate beeswax that the comb is made of, and you can then savor and swallow the sweet honey inside the cells. You can chew the wax into a little wad and remove it from your mouth. Some people prefer to swallow the wax, believing that it aids digestion, and there is no harm in this.

Honey buyers have a choice even among styles of comb honey. They can buy cut-comb honey, section-comb honey, or chunk honey. A piece of cut-comb honey is simply a square or rectangle sliced from a honeycomb. It comes wrapped in clear plastic or in a decorated cardboard box topped with a clear window.

Section comb honey gets its name from special little wooden frames, or "sections," that are put into hives for the bees to build their honeycomb in. The buyer gets the entire section, wood frame and all, just as the bees have filled it.

A 19th century bee master with a frame of honey.

Chunk honey is usually sold in wide-mouthed glass jars. A large piece of comb honey is put in each jar. Then the jar is filled to the brim with liquid honey.

Comb honey is delicious to eat and wonderful to look at—you can see the delicate, perfectly formed cells of the honeycomb as well as the lovely tint of the honey. But most people in the United States prefer their honey without beeswax, so most of the honey sold here is in liquid form.

How pure is the honey you buy? Before the federal government passed the Pure Food Law in 1906, honey was sometimes diluted with water or sugar syrup. But today the government sets strict standards for honey processing. And the United States Department of Agriculture assigns all honey a grade. There are four grades, each of which may be described in either of two ways:

U.S. Grade A, or U.S. Fancy
U.S. Grade B, or U.S. Choice
U.S. Grade C, or U.S. Standard
U.S. Grade D, or Substandard

Liquid honey described as Grade A has the best flavor, clarity, and consistency, and the greatest freedom from impurities. In the case of comb honey, Grade A means that the bees have filled and capped every cell on the comb.

In addition to U.S. Grade or country of origin (which may be indicated if the honey is imported), here are some other terms that you may see on a honey label:

Blended: This means that the honey does not come predominantly from one kind of flower. If it came mostly from clover, it would be called clover honey; if it came mostly from orange blossoms, it would be called orange-blossom honey. When no principal flower flavor is evident, the honey is often named in general terms—for example it may be called "wildflower" honey.

It is the bees, then, that do the blending as they collect their nectar from many flower sources. But sometimes the beekeeper, too, will blend different kinds of honey in order to achieve the flavor and thickness he desires. Some honeys, like Scottish heather honey, are so thick that they will not flow out of the jar when it is held upside down. To make them easier to spread, such honeys are often blended with thinner ones.

Filtered: This is honey that has been passed through a filter to remove pollen grains and fine particles of wax. Most honey sold in the United States has been filtered, though it is not required that the label say so, and most labels do not.

Unfiltered: This honey is sometimes passed through a very coarse filter but it still contains pollen, which gives it a slightly cloudy look. Most home-produced honeys and European honeys are treated this way.

Organic: This is supposed to mean that the honey was made from the nectar of plants grown without the use of chemical fertilizers or pesticides. But there is no way to confine bees to organically farmed land.

Raw: Honey that has not been heated but has been passed through a very coarse filter, or has not been filtered at all. This honey may granulate, but can be reliquified easily and without affecting its delicate flavor by following the procedure on page 92.

Natural: This term is inserted solely for its sales appeal. All honey is natural.

You may be able to find several different kinds of honey at your supermarket, and additional kinds at local gourmet and health food stores. Still other unusual and delightful honeys can be ordered by mail. Here is a list of suppliers and the special honeys that they offer.

 WHERE TO BUY UNUSUAL HONEYS

Api-Centro
Apolo. 5118
Lima 1, Peru

Suppliers of mango honey, avocado honey, and banana honey (from Peru).

Bee-King Enterprises
P.O. Box 9429
809 Frederick Road
Catonville, Maryland 21228

Suppliers of tupelo honey, orange blossom honey, and creamed orange blossom honey (from Florida); blueberry blossom honey (from New Jersey); and tulip poplar and creamed tulip poplar honey (from Maryland).

The Brookstone Company
40 Vose Farm Road
Petersborough,
New Hampshire 03458

Suppliers of jungle honey (from Central America), buckwheat honey (from New York State and Canada), thyme honey (from Mt. Hymettus, Greece), huajillo honey (from Texas), and forest honey (from Germany).

Desert Dawn Distributors
4746 East Grant Road
Tucson, Arizona 85712

Suppliers of cat's claw honey, mesquite honey, and desert flower honey (from Arizona).

Glenmont Woods Honey Farm
6137 Ely Road
Wooster, Ohio 44691

Suppliers of cut-comb black locust honey and fine creamed honey (from Ohio).

Goleta Honey and Bee Supply
6409-D Camino Vista
Goleta, California 93017

Suppliers of black button sage comb honey, orange blossom honey, wildflower honey, avocado honey, buckwheat honey, and clover honey (from California).

Home Rule Natural Foods
1825 Columbia Road, N.W.
Washington, D.C. 20009

Suppliers of leatherwood honey (from Tasmania), lotus blossom honey (from New Zealand), lime blossom and acacia blossom honeys (from Romania), heather honey (from Germany), eucalyptus honey and tamarisk honey (from California), and wildflower honey (from Mexico).

Oneota Valley Apiary
Route 4
Decorah, Iowa

Suppliers of a light-colored, mild-flavored honey made mostly from basswood and yellow clover blossoms (from Iowa).

Pooh Corner
P.O. Box 638
Micanopy, Florida 32667

Suppliers of royal palm honey, citrus honey, wildflower honey, and gallberry honey (from Florida).

Solarius Honey Company
RR 3
Box 319
Mountain View, Missouri 65548

Suppliers of Ozark Mountain wildflower honey. (The nectar for this honey comes mostly from blackberry blossoms.)

A beehive inspired this elaborate cake.

CHAPTER TWELVE

Cooking with Honey

He who deals with honey will sometimes be licking his fingers.

—Old Proverb

BESIDES being a delicious food all by itself, honey is a wonderful ingredient in a wide variety of dishes. Here—following some general hints for cooking with honey—is a specially chosen assortment of honey recipes. Some have come down to us from the ancient world, some from the Middle Ages, and some are from the national cuisines of the peoples of the world today.

I hope you will try them out. Honey is something you can learn about only partly from reading. For the other part, you'll need to use your knife, fork, and spoon.

Cooking with Honey: Hints

1. Honey will not spoil.

2. Store honey in a dry place. Do not refrigerate it. Refrigeration will hasten granulation.

3. If the honey does granulate, place the jar in a pan of water and put it in an oven set at 200 degrees. Remove the honey as soon as it reliquifies.

4. Tip for measuring honey: oil or butter the measuring cup or spoon before filling it with honey. This will prevent the honey from sticking to it.

5. Warming honey slightly, by placing the jar in a larger container of hot water for a few minutes, makes it easier to pour.

6. Baked goods made with honey are often more tasty if you wrap and store them for a few days before serving, to allow the flavor time to develop.

7. Honey candies should be kept in an airtight container to keep them from becoming sticky.

8. Twelve ounces of honey by weight equal eight ounces—one measuring cup—by volume.

9. If cookies made with honey are too hard, you can soften them by putting them in an airtight container with a slice of peeled apple.

10. *Please note:* be very careful when you are heating honey. Honey foams up when it reaches boiling. Hot honey can cause a painful burn.

Substituting Honey for Sugar

Honey can be substituted for sugar in almost any recipe. Just keep in mind the following rules:

1. When substituting honey for sugar in a recipe, add 1 cup of honey in place of each cup of sugar called for, and reduce the amount of liquid in the recipe by ¼ cup for each cup of honey added.

2. Recipes containing honey need to be beaten longer and more vigorously than sugar recipes.

3. When substituting honey for sugar in a recipe for baked goods, add ½ teaspoon baking soda for each cup of honey used and lower the baking temperature by 25 degrees. Honey batter becomes crisp and brown faster than sugar batter.

A Few More Ideas

* Use your imagination at all times—the uses of honey are almost limitless. For instance, a teaspoonful added to cooked vegetables, a minute or two before they are finished cooking, will enhance their flavor.

* Honey can be used to sweeten any drink. It combines well with hot or cold liquids. Simply stir it in.

* Honey is easily dispensed from a plastic squeeze container that can be left on the table like a sugar bowl.

* Adding a tablespoonful of honey to a cake mix will improve the flavor of the cake. Just omit 1 teaspoonful of the liquid.

The Four Elements, by Sébastien Shopff.

*Honey butter is a delicious spread for toast, pancakes, or waffles. Soften ½ cup of butter by leaving it at room temperature for a few minutes. Add ½ cup of honey and blend well with a fork. Chicken and fish baked in honey butter are especially good.

*Cold drinks can be flavored with honey ice cubes. Blend ½ cup honey into 2 cups of hot water. Squeeze in a teaspoonful of fresh lemon juice. Cool and freeze in ice cube trays.

*Whisk honey into your favorite sauces just before serving. Honey adds color and flavor.

*Experiment with a variety of honeys. A spicy herb honey or a delicate flower honey will lend different flavors to your recipes.

THE ANCIENT WORLD

Prehistoric man ate his honey straight from the comb. But as civilizations developed, so did ways of serving honey: hot and cold, in sauces and in salads, with meat and with fish, in breads and in cakes—in fact, in almost every form and combined with almost every ingredient imaginable.

A few written recipes have survived from ancient times. They were preserved on clay tablets from Egypt, scribbled on kitchen walls at Pompeii—some are even in cookbook form. But most of what we know about cookery in the distant past comes from the texts of ancient historians and poets, and from the excavations of archeologists.

In Sumer, in Babylon, and in ancient Egypt, ordinary people lived on a kind of porridge made with grain. Only

Some Roman cooking utensils.

occasionally were their meals enlivened with bits of meat or fruit. Honey, when it was available, was a delicious way of sweetening the eternal porridge.

Rich people in Egypt—probably the land where cooks first learned how to make bread rise—ate a special bread made mostly from flour and honey. This they sculpted into animal, bird, or insect shapes before it was baked.

Honey from Mount Hymettus in Greece was famous throughout the ancient world. The Greeks added it to foods as different as wine, porridge, fish, and salad.

The Greeks and Romans shared many eating habits, but Greek banquets never matched the lavish extremes of Imperial Rome. Rich Romans dined on the most exotic and expensive food obtainable. Fantastic pastry animals and birds, ostrich brains, peacock tongues, costly spices like black pepper, and fruits from faraway lands were their daily fare. And they ate hugely—at a Roman banquet, course followed course until the participants could eat no more. Romans favored spicy sauces of honey and vinegar, and sipped a mixture of honey and wine at nearly every meal. As a guest departed he was often presented with a gift, perhaps toothpaste made of ashes of dogs' teeth and honey. And if he wished to sweeten his breath, he used a mouthwash of anise, wine, and honey.

The following recipes from ancient times combine honey with yogurt, peas, cheese, dates, and seeds. They are easy to make and delicious to eat.

Pasteli   Roman Dates
   (Greek Sesame Seed Candy)   Panchamrit (Yogurt Drink)
Honeyed Cheesecakes
Peas à la Vitellius
   (Peas in an Egg Sauce)

PASTELI

GREEK SESAME SEED CANDY

Sesame seeds are the oldest seeds known to have been used as spices in cooking. This sesame honey candy was made in Greece thousands of years ago.

½ pound orange blossom honey   *orange water* *
½ pound sesame seeds

Put the honey in a heavy saucepan and cook over medium heat for 15 minutes. Stir in the sesame seeds. Continue cooking, stirring constantly, for five minutes.

Pour a little orange water on a tray or marble board. Tilt it several times so that the whole tray is moistened. Pour on the honey mixture and spread it to a thickness of ½ inch. Let the candy cool at room temperature. Cut it into 1-inch squares. Turn the pieces with a spatula and let them dry on a rack for 2 or 3 hours. Store between layers of waxed paper in an airtight container.   *About 3 dozen pieces.*

*Orange water can be purchased at specialty food stores, or plain water may be substituted.

HONEYED CHEESECAKES

Ancient Greek writers wrote lovingly of honeyed cheese-cakes. It is easy to understand their enthusiasm.

½ cup water	*3 eggs*
¾ cup honey	*½ cup flour*
2 cups cottage cheese	*salt*
½ teaspoon almond extract	*½ cup chopped almonds*

Prepare a syrup by bringing the water and ¼ cup honey to a boil. Reduce heat, and simmer for 5 minutes. Let the syrup cool.

Preheat the oven to 350.° Place cupcake papers in a 12-muffin tin.

With the back of a spoon, press the cottage cheese through a strainer into a large bowl. Add ½ cup honey and the almond extract. Mix well. Beat in the eggs, one at a time. Stir in the flour and a pinch of salt. Mix the almonds into the batter and pour it into muffin tins, filling the papers to the top.

Bake until the tops are puffed and golden and a toothpick inserted into the centers comes out clean, about 45 minutes. Spoon honey syrup over the hot cakes. Cool in the tin. The cakes will shrink slightly. Put them on a platter and chill in the refrigerator for 2 to 3 hours before serving. *12 cakes.*

PANCHAMRIT
YOGURT DRINK

A beverage that has been drunk in India for hundreds of years in a religious ceremony on *Purnamasi*, the day of the full moon.

½ cup yogurt	*melted butter, a few drops*
½ cup milk	*3 or 4 ice cubes*
1 cup cold water	*1 teaspoon ground pistachio nuts*
3 tablespoons honey	*2 or 3 pieces of rock candy*

Mix the yogurt, milk, water, and honey. Beat in the melted butter with a fork. Add 3 or 4 ice cubes and continue to beat until the mixture is foamy.

Stir in the ground pistachio nuts and pieces of rock candy and serve at once.   *2 servings.*

ROMAN DATES

This recipe comes from the only surviving Roman cookbook. Its legendary author, Apicius, was said to have poisoned himself when he realized that he had only about three-quarters of a ton of gold bullion left to his name—not enough, he feared, to maintain a decent standard of living.

20 dates	*salt*
20 whole almonds	*½ cup honey*
black pepper	

Remove the pits from the dates.

Sprinkle the almonds with freshly ground black pepper and stuff one into each date.

Spread a thin layer of salt on a tray. Roll the dates, one at a time, in the salt. Put them in a heavy saucepan. Pour the honey over the dates and bring to a boil. Reduce the heat and simmer 3 minutes.

Spoon the warm dates and sauce into individual serving dishes. *4 servings.*

PEAS À LA VITELLIUS
PEAS IN AN EGG SAUCE

Aulus Vitellius was a Roman Emperor who had a reputation for extreme gluttony. This unusual dish of peas in a spicy egg sauce is named after him. Another of his favorite dishes combined peas with pearls and gold pieces.

½ cup water
2 cups fresh or frozen peas
2 yolks of hard-boiled eggs
½ teaspoon ground black pepper
⅛ teaspoon ground ginger

¼ teaspoon salt
2 tablespoons honey
1 teaspoon wine vinegar
1 tablespoon oil

Bring ½ cup water to a boil. Add the peas and reduce the heat. Simmer, covered, until tender, about 15 minutes. (If you are using frozen peas, follow the directions on the package.) If the water boils away during cooking, add more. Drain the cooked peas, cover to keep warm, and put aside.

While the peas are cooking, mash the egg yolks with the black pepper, ginger, and salt. Add the honey, wine vinegar, and oil. Beat until smooth. Put the mixture in a small saucepan and bring to a boil. Remove from heat, toss with the peas, and serve.   *4 servings.*

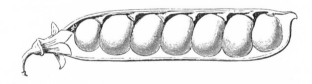

THE MIDDLE AGES

In the Middle Ages, more people drank honey, in the form of mead, than ate it. Like honey itself, this honey wine was thought to have numerous healthful effects. It nourished infants and rejuvenated the aged; it cooled fevers; it healed sores—or so people believed.

Howell the Good, a tenth-century historian, records that the Mead-Maker was the eleventh most important official in the royal court of Wales. This honorable personage received his land and horses as a royal gift, his woolen clothing from the king, and his linen clothing from the queen—as well as part of the mead he produced.

Huge supplies of mead were often kept on hand in medieval villages. This is illustrated by a legend about the German town of Meissen, where there is said to have been a dangerous drought in the year 1015. Just when the water supply was lowest, a fierce fire broke out. But the towns-people were able to extinguish it by pouring on their enormous supplies of mead.

Of course, honey was important as a food, too. It was used in cakes and sauces, and also as a preservative for meat, fruit, and eggs. Catherine de Medici, who was married to King Henry II of France, had fish imported from her native Italy packed in vessels of honey.

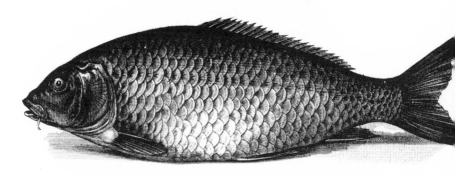

Italy also exported honeycakes to France, until a rumor started that Catherine was a poisoner. Then the French became afraid that the Italians were mixing poison into the cakes, and stopped buying them. Not until Catherine left the throne did honeycakes again become popular in France.

Medieval bakers all over Europe used honey in spice cakes. These "cakes" were actually small cookie-like creations of flour, spices, and honey. They had marvelous keeping powers. On certain special occasions, in fact, these long-lasting cakes were intended as mementos rather than food. For instance, a girl might give a heart-shaped one to her sweetheart, who was going off to war, as a forget-me-not. Such a cake might have a little inlaid mirror, and tender sayings carved around the edges.

Other honeycakes were meant as funeral souvenirs. They were passed around after the ceremony to those in attendance. Each little cake carried a portrait of the dead person pressed into the dough.

For more light-hearted occasions, cakes were shaped to resemble animals, flowers, or birds. The most elaborate ones were actually painted with gold leaf.

Almost every country in Europe had its favorite honey dishes. A sampling of them is included among the recipes that follow.

Golden Apples (Spiced Meatballs) Cameline Sauce
Rysbred (Rice Pancakes) Frumenty (Wheat Pudding)
Douce Âme (Capon in Milk and Nurembergers (Honey Cookies)
  Honey)

GOLDEN APPLES
SPICED MEATBALLS

Medieval cooks enjoyed "painting" food vivid colors with vegetable dyes to fool the diner about what he was getting to eat. Foods were most often tinted gold, the color of royalty. These bright yellow "apples" are carefully decorated meatballs mixed with raisins and spices.

½ cup raisins	3 egg yolks
1 pound ground beef	½ teaspoon ground saffron or
½ teaspoon salt	3 drops yellow food coloring
½ teaspoon ground nutmeg	3 tablespoons flour
½ teaspoon ground cloves	3 tablespoons honey
1 pinch cayenne pepper	cinnamon
1 egg, beaten	

Preheat the oven to 375°.

Mix the raisins, ground beef, salt, nutmeg, cloves, cayenne, and the beaten egg. Form the mixture into 8 round balls. Place on a rack in a baking pan. Bake 20 minutes. Remove from the oven and chill in the refrigerator for 30 minutes.

Beat the egg yolks, saffron, and flour to make a thick paste. Use a knife to spread it evenly over the chilled balls. Replace them on the rack and bake 15 minutes longer.

Put the cooked meatballs on a serving platter. For a "stem," stick a clove in the top of each ball. Drizzle honey over them. Sprinkle with cinnamon and serve.   *4 servings.*

RYSBRED
RICE PANCAKES

Pancakes were popular at every meal in the Middle Ages. These unusual, crunchy, delicately flavored pancakes have a spicy honey topping.

2 ½ cups water
1 cup rice
4 tablespoons oil
2 onions
1 tablespoon flour
½ teaspoon ground mace

½ teaspoon salt
¼ cup chopped almonds
2 eggs
2 tablespoons dark honey
½ teaspoon ground cinnamon

Bring the water to a boil. Add the rice. Reduce heat and sim-

mer, covered, until the water is absorbed, about 25 minutes. Set aside to cool.

Heat 2 tablespoons oil in a heavy frying pan. Chop and add the onions. Sauté until golden. Remove from the pan and cool. Leave the excess oil in the pan.

Mix the flour, mace, salt, and almonds. Stir the mixture into the cooked rice. Beat in the eggs. Mix thoroughly.

Add 2 tablespoons of oil to the frying pan and place over medium heat. When the pan is hot, drop in tablespoonfuls of batter. Cook until golden brown. Turn and cook the other side. Drain on paper towels. Transfer to a serving platter.

Mix the cinnamon and honey and spread it over the pancakes. Serve warm. *14 to 16 pancakes.*

DOUCE ÂME
CAPON IN MILK AND HONEY

Milk, honey, spices, and long, slow cooking produce tender chicken in a flavorful sauce. Saffron turns it the golden color medieval diners so admired. Douce Âme was popular at the court of Richard II.

one 7 to 8 pound capon or two	½ cup honey
3 to 4 pound chickens, cut up	3 tablespoons chopped parsley
1 cup flour	½ teaspoon ground sage
1 teaspoon salt	1 teaspoon ground savory
½ teaspoon black pepper	1 teaspoon ground saffron
¼ cup oil	(optional)
3 cups milk	⅔ cup chopped walnuts

Put the capon or chicken pieces in a heavy bag with flour, salt, and pepper. Shake until well coated. Heat the oil in a large frying pan. Add and brown the chicken pieces on both sides.

Mix the milk, honey, parsley, sage, savory, and saffron. Pour over the browned chicken or capon pieces in the frying pan. Cover, reduce heat, and simmer for 1½ hours over very low heat. Remove the frying pan from the heat and transfer the chicken and sauce to a serving platter. Sprinkle the walnuts over the chicken.   *6 to 8 servings.*

FRUMENTY
WHEAT PUDDING

A nutritious pudding that was sometimes enriched with bits of meat. Frumenty was so popular in the Middle Ages that some historians believe it was eaten more often than bread.

1 ¾ cups milk	1 cup cracked wheat
½ teaspoon almond extract	1 egg yolk
2 tablespoons honey	ground saffron (optional)

Mix the milk, almond extract, and honey in a heavy saucepan. Bring to a boil. Add the cracked wheat and reduce the heat to low. Cover and cook, stirring occasionally, until the liquid is absorbed, about 15 minutes. Remove from the heat. Stir in the egg yolk. Add a pinch of saffron and mix well. Serve hot or cold.

4 servings.

NUREMBERGERS
HONEY COOKIES

In the Middle Ages, the German city of Nuremberg was a trading center for spices from the Orient. Imported spices and native honey were joined in these pretty, flowerlike cookies.

1 cup honey	½ teaspoon ground allspice
2 eggs	½ teaspoon ground cloves
1 tablespoon lemon juice	½ cup chopped almonds
grated rind of ½ lemon	½ cup chopped candied orange
3 cups flour	peel*
1 teaspoon baking soda	candied lemon peel*
½ teaspoon ground cinnamon	sliced almonds

*A recipe for candied orange or lemon peel appears on page 130. Or you may substitute fresh, grated peel.

Beat together the honey, eggs, lemon juice, and grated lemon rind. Mix the flour, baking soda, cinnamon, allspice, and cloves, and stir into the egg mixture. Add the almonds and candied orange peel to the dough. Mix well. Wrap the dough in tinfoil and chill in the refrigerator for 12 hours or overnight.

Preheat the oven to 350°.

Flour your hands. Quickly roll generous teaspoonfuls of dough into balls and flatten them between your palms. Reflour your hands whenever they feel sticky. Decorate the cookies to look like flowers. Press a small circle of candied lemon peel into the center of each cookie and surround it with petals made from sliced almonds.

Grease and flour a cookie sheet. Place the cookies 2 inches apart on the sheet. Bake until they are puffed and firm, about 10 minutes. Remove them with a spatula and cook on racks. Store the cookies in an airtight container for several days to allow the flavor to develop before eating.   *4 dozen cookies.*

Printed for Rich: Lownes

CAMELINE SAUCE

Spicy, colorful sauces were used to decorate, flavor, and sometimes to disguise the taste of spoiled meat and fish. This spiced cinnamon sauce was as popular in England and France in the fourteenth century as ketchup is today.

⅛ teaspoon crushed red pepper
3 cups beef stock or broth
3 tablespoons honey
1 tablespoon wine vinegar
2 cinnamon sticks
½ teaspoon whole cloves
½ teaspoon ground ginger
½ teaspoon whole black
   peppercorns
½ teaspoon ground mace
2 cups fresh whole wheat bread,
   crumbled
salt
ground cinnamon

Put the crushed red pepper, beef stock, honey, wine vinegar, cinnamon sticks, whole cloves, ginger, black peppers, and mace in a heavy saucepan. Bring to a boil. Reduce the heat and simmer, covered, for 15 minutes. Add the crumbled bread and cook over low heat, stirring occasionally, for 30 minutes longer. Pour the sauce through a strainer, carefully pressing out all the liquid. Discard the bread. Add salt to taste. Pour into a gravy pitcher, sprinkle lightly with ground cinnamon, and serve with roast meat. *1½ cups.*

AROUND THE WORLD

People all over the world have created wonderful honey recipes that reflect their traditions of eating. Here are some interesting ones, chosen from many different countries, for you to prepare and enjoy.

Scottish Honey Scones
Bircher Muesli (Swiss Cereal)
Mehalis (Orange Rice)
Oen Cymreig Melog (Welsh Honeyed Lamb)
Genoese Chestnut Hot Pot
Sweet and Sour Spareribs
Tzimmes (Meat and Vegetable Stew)
Arabian Chicken
Brazilian Yogurt Cream
Spiced Acorn Squash
Csalla Mary (Hungarian Salad)
Honey Icing

Russian Beet Jam
Candied Orange or Lemon Peel
Rose Honey
Fig Bread
Oatcakes
Pain d'Épices (Honey Bread)
Scripture Cake
Honey Jumbles (Cookies)
Lekach (Honeycake)
Algerian Charlotte
Aish-el-Saraya (Egyptian Palace Bread)
Fruit Compote
Peanut Butter Balls

Charoses (Apple-Nut relish)
Honeyed Nahit (Baked Chick-
peas)
Honey Glazed Carrots
Honey Bran Muffins

Honey Custard
Meli Pita (Honey Pie)
Spicy Oranges
Scandinavian Fruit Soup

A man-faced beehive made of straw.

SCOTTISH HONEY SCONES

Flat, round, tasty, little scones that take only a few minutes to prepare and bake. They are delicious with butter and honey. In Scotland they are served at teatime.

1 cup flour	*1 egg*
¼ teaspoon salt	*3 tablespoons honey*
2 teaspoons baking powder	*½ cup raisins*
3 tablespoons butter, softened	*milk*

Preheat the oven to 425°.

Mix the flour, salt, and baking powder. Add the butter with a fork, stirring well. The mixture will be crumbly.

Beat the egg lightly and stir in the honey. Add to the flour mixture. Then stir in the raisins. Form the dough into a ball.

Flour a board. Roll out the dough with a rolling pin to a thickness of ½ inch. Cut out the scones with a 2-inch cookie cutter. Brush the top of each scone lightly with milk.

Grease a cookie sheet and sprinkle it with flour. Place the scones 1 inch apart. Bake until the tops are browned, about 10 minutes. Transfer to a rack to cool. *16 to 18 scones.*

BIRCHER MUESLI
SWISS CEREAL

Dr. Bircher Benner, who founded a health clinic in Zurich, Switzerland, in 1897, created this dish. It became the rage in his country and is now a favorite American breakfast.

3 tablespoons oatmeal *
2 tablespoons cold water
2 tablespoons fresh lemon juice
6 tablespoons plain yogurt

2 tablespoons honey
2 apples
2 tablespoons finely chopped nuts

Soak the oatmeal in the water for 8 to 12 hours. Mix in the lemon juice, yogurt, and honey.

Grate the apples, discarding the seeds and core. Stir the apples and nuts into the cereal. Blend and serve at once.

1 serving.

MEHALIS
ORANGE RICE

This Moorish dish from North Africa is a soft, orange-flavored rice. Try it at breakfast, instead of cereal.

1 cup rice
1 cup water
1½ cups milk
2 tablespoons honey

2 tablespoons butter
1 tablespoon orange juice
1 teaspoon grated orange peel

Bring the rice and water to a boil in a heavy saucepan. Boil gently until the rice softens, about 5 minutes. Add the milk, cover, and simmer 20 minutes longer. Stir in the honey. Bring to a boil and continue to boil, uncovered, for 3 minutes. Stir in the butter, orange juice, and orange peel. Boil 5 minutes longer. Serve hot or cold.

4 to 6 servings.

* Do not use instant oatmeal.

OEN CYMREIG MELOG
WELSH HONEYED LAMB

Wales produces excellent lamb and fine honey. They are used to great advantage in this superb Welsh specialty.

3 to 4 pound leg of lamb	*2 tablespoons rosemary*
salt and pepper	*1 cup light honey*
2 teaspoons ground ginger	*1 ½ cups apple cider*

Preheat the oven to 450°. Grease a roasting pan.

Sprinkle the lamb with salt, pepper, ginger, and rosemary. Place it in the roasting pan. Spoon ⅔ cup honey over the top. Pour 1 cup of cider around the lamb in the pan. Mix the remaining honey and cider in a small bowl. Use it to baste the meat frequently.

Place the roasting pan in the oven and reduce the heat to 400°. Cook the meat to taste, using an oven thermometer. Rare meat will register 140°, and take about 12 minutes for each pound. Well-done meat will register 175° and take about 18 minutes for each pound. When the meat is cooked as you like it, transfer to a serving platter. Pour the pan juices into a small pitcher and serve with the meat as gravy.   *6 to 8 servings.*

TZIMMES

MEAT AND VEGETABLE STEW

Depending on local supplies and customs, East European cooks prepare many variations of this slow-cooking honeyed stew. Beans, rice, raisins, celery, and spices are sometimes included.

2 to 3 pound brisket of beef	*2 tablespoons oil*
6 carrots	*2 cups prunes, pitted*
2 large sweet potatoes	*½ cup honey*

Cut the fat off the brisket. Cut the meat into 1-inch cubes. Wash and slice the carrots. Peel the sweet potatoes and dice them.

Heat 2 tablespoons of oil in a large, heavy pot. Add and brown the beef over medium heat. Add the carrots, sweet potatoes, prunes, honey, and enough water to cover the food. Bring to a boil. Then reduce the heat and simmer, covered, until the meat is very tender, about 2½ hours.   *4 to 6 servings.*

GENOESE CHESTNUT HOT POT

This North Italian dish is an unusual blend of sweet and savory textures. Serve it as a main course with crusty Italian bread.

2 pounds pears	*½ pound chestnuts*
3 cups water	*1 cup milk*
1 stick cinnamon	*2 tablespoons whole wheat flour*
4 cloves	*2 tablespoons honey*
½ teaspoon salt	*4 slices bacon*

Peel and core the pears. Cut them in quarters. Bring 2 cups of water to a boil. Add the pears, cinnamon, and cloves. Reduce the heat and simmer, covered, until the fruit is tender, about 30 minutes. Remove the cinnamon stick. Drain the pears and set aside.

While the pears are cooking, bring 1 cup water and ½ teaspoon salt to a boil. Add the chestnuts and boil until tender, about 15 minutes. Drain, peel off the shells and skins, and add the chestnuts to the cooked pears. Put the mixture in a heavy saucepan.

Beat the milk, flour, and honey until smooth. Stir into the pear mixture. Mash the mixture slightly with a fork.

Cook the bacon in a frying pan until it is crisp. Remove with a spatula and drain on paper towels. Crumble the bacon and stir into the pear mixture. Cover and cook over very low heat, stirring occasionally, for 30 minutes. Spoon into bowls and serve.

4 servings.

Some beekeepers created elaborate hives like this wooden one in the shape of a woman.

ARABIAN CHICKEN

A crisp, crusty, candied skin distinguishes this tasty roasted chicken.

4 tablespoons butter	*3 to 4 pound roasting chicken*
4 tablespoons honey	*½ cup chopped nuts*
1 tablespoon lemon juice	

Preheat the oven to 450°.

Melt the butter in a small saucepan. Add the honey and lemon juice, stirring until smooth. Remove from the heat.

Place the chicken on a roasting pan. Spoon the honey mixture all over it, inside and out, reserving about ¼ cup. Put the chicken in the oven. Reduce the heat to 350°. Bake 20 minutes for each pound of chicken, basting often with the leftover honey mixture. When the chicken is cooked, sprinkle with the chopped nuts and serve. *3 to 4 servings.*

SWEET AND SOUR SPARERIBS

Chinese cooks are famous for their delicate sweet and sour sauces. These spareribs are enhanced by a honeyed vegetable sauce.

½ cup honey	*½ cup peanut oil*
2 tablespoons vinegar	*3 tablespoons cornstarch*
1 carrot	*3 tablespoons water*
1 tomato	*1 cup pineapple chunks*
1 green pepper	*2 pounds spareribs, cut in 1-inch pieces*

Mix the honey and vinegar. Set aside. Grate the carrot. Chop the tomato. Remove the seeds from the green pepper and chop it. Heat 2 tablespoons peanut oil in a heavy skillet. Add the vegetables and cook over medium heat, stirring often, until they are soft. Stir in the honey and vinegar mixture.

Stir the cornstarch into 3 tablespoons of water. Add to the vegetables and cook over low heat, stirring often, until the sauce thickens. Gently stir in the pineapple chunks. Remove the food from the skillet, cover to keep warm, and set aside. Wash and dry the skillet.

Heat the remaining peanut oil in the skillet. Add the spareribs to the hot oil and cook, stirring, until they are well browned. Remove from the pan, drain on paper towels, and put into a serving dish. Pour the vegetable sauce on top. Serve at once.

4 servings.

A Chinese sweetmeat vendor.

SPICED ACORN SQUASH

Squash is a native American vegetable. Here is an easy and delicious recipe for baked acorn squash.

2 acorn squashes	*1 teaspoon salt*
8 tablespoons honey	*4 tablespoons butter*
½ teaspoon ground cinnamon	

Preheat the oven to 375°.

Cut the acorn squashes in half. Scoop out the seeds and soft pulp that clings to them, and discard. Fill each half with 2 tablespoons of honey, ⅛ teaspoon of cinnamon, ¼ teaspoon of salt, and 1 tablespoon butter. Pour hot water into a baking pan to a depth of ½ inch. Arrange the halves in the pan. Bake 1¼ hours.

Serves 4.

A kitchen scene from the sketchbook of Pennsylvania German folk artist Lewis Miller, around 1799.

BRAZILIAN YOGURT CREAM

The velvet-smooth yogurt sauce contrasts pleasantly in texture with the crisp cucumbers. Serve as a salad or an appetizer.

2 cucumbers	*1½ cups plain yogurt*
2 sprigs parsley	*2 tablespoons honey*
1 clove garlic	*salt and pepper*

Wash and dry the cucumbers. Cut them into thin slices. Put the slices in a bowl of salt water for five minutes. Drain and dry them thoroughly.

Chop the parsley. Peel and crush the garlic. Mix the parsley, garlic, yogurt, honey, and a sprinkling of salt and pepper to taste. Beat until smooth. Stir in the cucumber slices.

Chill for 3 or 4 hours before serving. *4 to 6 servings.*

CSALLA MARY
HUNGARIAN SALAD

Spicy coleslaw with a clear, flavorful honey dressing.

1 white cabbage	*1 cucumber*
2 tomatoes	*2 tablespoons white vinegar*
1 sour pickle	*⅓ cup olive oil*
1 onion	*2 tablespoons fresh lemon juice*
1 red pepper	*2 tablespoons honey*
1 green pepper	*1 teaspoon salt*

Grate the cabbage, tomatoes, pickle, onion, red and green peppers, and cucumber. Toss them together in a salad bowl.

Mix the vinegar, oil, lemon juice, honey, and salt. Beat until smooth. Pour the mixture over the salad and toss until it is thoroughly coated. *8 servings.*

HONEY GLAZED CARROTS

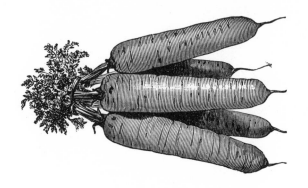

A fancy touch for a favorite vegetable.

½ cup water	*2 tablespoons butter*
3 cups thinly sliced carrots	*2 tablespoons honey*

Bring ½ cup of water to a boil. Add the sliced carrots. Cover, reduce heat, and simmer until tender, about 20 minutes. Drain.

Melt the butter in a heavy frying pan over low heat. Stir in the honey. Add the carrots and cook, stirring, until they are well coated with the honey mixture.   *4 to 6 servings.*

CHAROSES

APPLE-NUT RELISH

Charoses is served at Passover, the Jewish holiday that celebrates the release of the Hebrews from slavery in Egypt. Cinnamon gives the mixture the color of the red bricks that they hauled and carried as slaves. The red wine is to suggest the Red Sea, which they crossed to escape.

2 cups chopped apples   2 tablespoons honey
¼ cup chopped almonds   ½ teaspoon ground cinnamon
¼ cup chopped walnuts   2 tablespoons red wine
½ teaspoon grated lemon rind

Mix the apples, almonds, walnuts, lemon rind, honey, cinnamon, and wine. Stir gently. Store in the refrigerator. Serve on matzos or crackers. *Serves 8 to 10.*

HONEYED NAHIT
BAKED CHICKPEAS

Chickpeas have been a popular food of Middle Eastern people for centuries. This simple dish is nourishing and tasty.

2 cups chickpeas   ½ cup honey
3 tablespoons butter   ⅓ cup water
1½ teaspoons salt   2 teaspoons lemon juice

Put the chickpeas in a bowl. Cover with cold water and soak overnight. In the morning, drain the chickpeas. Put them in a heavy saucepan. Add enough water to cover and bring the chickpeas to a boil. Reduce heat, cover, and simmer 1½ hours. If the water boils away, add more. Drain the cooked chickpeas and put them in a shallow casserole dish.

Preheat the oven to 350°.

Melt the butter. Mix it with the salt, honey, water, and lemon juice. Pour the mixture over the chickpeas. Bake in the oven for 30 minutes. *6 to 8 servings.*

Following page: An elegant French kitchen of the 19th century.

CANDIED ORANGE OR LEMON PEEL

Candied peel makes a lovely decoration for cakes and cookies. It is an ingredient in several of the recipes in this book. It can also be served as a sweet by itself.

4 oranges or 8 lemons   *1 ⅓ cups honey*
12 cups water

Cut the fruit into quarters. Peel each quarter. Cut off from the peel as much as possible of the white inner skin.

Bring 4 cups of cold water to a boil in a heavy saucepan. Add the peels. Turn the heat to low, cover, and simmer 15 minutes. Drain the water, leaving the peels in the pot. Add 4 fresh cups of cold water and bring to a boil. Turn the heat to low, cover, and simmer 15 minutes. Drain, and once more add 4 cups cold water. Bring to a boil, reduce heat, and simmer 15 minutes. Remove the cooked peel and cut each piece into 3 slices, lengthwise. Set aside.

Put the honey in a saucepan and bring it to a boil. Add the sliced peels and stir to coat them well. Reduce the heat to low and simmer 45 minutes, stirring occasionally. Remove the pan from the heat and cool the peels in the honey. Put the cooled peels on wire racks. Let them dry 12 hours, turning occasionally. Store them in an airtight container.   *1 cup.*

ROSE HONEY

Martha Washington is credited with the recipe for this delicately flavored honey. Serve it as a spread or try it in Honey
Custard, page 144.

1 cup honey   ½ cup fresh rose petals*

Bring the honey to a boil in a heavy saucepan. Be careful that
the honey does not boil over. Turn off the heat as soon as the
honey starts to foam up. Stir in the rose petals. Let the mixture
sit for four hours. Bring it to a boil again. Turn off the heat and
cool the honey in the pan. Pour it through a strainer. Discard the
petals. Store the honey in a covered jar.   *1 cup.*

*Use only petals from rose bushes that you know have not been sprayed
with chemicals.

RUSSIAN BEET JAM

A sweet, spicy sauce that complements cold meat or chicken.

1 pound beets   *1 to 2 teaspoons freshly grated*
honey   *ginger root or ½ to 1 teaspoon*
                                                ground ginger
                                      ½ cup sliced almonds

Wash the beets. Cut off the tops and stems. Put the beets in a saucepan with enough cold water to cover them. Bring the water to a boil, reduce heat, and simmer, covered for 1 hour. If the water boils away, add more. Drain, peel, and chop the beets. Pack them firmly into a measuring cup. Measure, and then return them to the saucepan. Measure an equal amount of honey and pour it over the beets. Cook over moderate heat, stirring often, until the mixture thickens. Remove from the heat. Grate, measure, and stir in the ginger to taste. Cool. Slice and measure the almonds. Stir them into the jam. Cover and store in the refrigerator. Serve cold.   *About 1 pint.*

FIG BREAD

Fresh figs and honey make this bread rich, moist, and delicious.

1 cup figs	*1 egg*
1 cup walnuts	*2 cups flour*
2 tablespoons oil	*1 teaspoon salt*
1 cup honey	*1 teaspoon baking powder*
1 teaspoon vanilla	*½ teaspoon baking soda*
¾ cup water	

Preheat the oven to 325°. Chop figs and walnuts.

Mix oil, honey, and vanilla. Boil ¾ cup water and stir it into the mixture. Add the figs. Cool. Beat in the egg.

Sift the flour, salt, baking powder, and baking soda. Add to the honey mixture and mix well. Stir in the walnuts.

Butter a 9-inch loaf pan. Pour in the batter. Bake until a toothpick inserted into the center comes out clean, about 1¼ hours. Cool pan on a rack for 5 minutes. Remove the bread from the pan and finish cooling on the rack.   *1 loaf.*

OATCAKES

These little cakes were useful to Scottish travelers because they kept well and were easy to stuff into pockets for a journey.

1 tablespoon butter	*1 teaspoon baking soda*
1 tablespoon water	*1 cup oat flour**
2 tablespoons honey	*½ cup milk*
¼ teaspoon salt	

*To make oat flour at home, grind rolled oats in the blender. Measure 1 cup.

Preheat the oven to 325°. Butter a cookie sheet.

Melt the butter in a small saucepan. Stir in the water and honey. Remove from the heat.

Mix the salt, baking soda, and oat flour. Add the butter mixture and stir with a fork. The mixture will be mealy. Add the milk and stir until the batter is smooth. Drop teaspoonfuls of the batter 2 inches apart on a cookie sheet. Put the sheet into the oven and bake until golden, about 10 minutes. Remove the cakes with a spatula and cool on racks. Store the oatcakes in an airtight container. *About 30 cakes.*

PAIN D'ÉPICES
HONEY BREAD

In French, it means gingerbread. This spicy bread is a specialty of Dijon, France. It is usually toasted and eaten with butter and jam.

1 cup water	*½ teaspoon ground mace*
1 cup dark honey	*½ teaspoon ground ginger*
3 tablespoons baking powder	*¼ teaspoon salt*
1½ teaspoons baking soda	*½ cup candied orange peel* *
1 teaspoon ground cloves	*4 cups flour*

Boil 1 cup water. Pour it into a large bowl. Add the honey, baking powder, baking soda, cloves, mace, ginger, and salt. Stir in the candied orange peel. Add the flour and mix well. Cover the batter and let it stand in a dry place for at least 1 hour.

Preheat the oven to 325°. Butter two 7-inch loaf pans. Divide the batter between them, spreading the tops evenly with a knife. Bake until the tops are browned and a toothpick inserted into the centers comes out clean, about 1 hour. *2 loaves.*

*See the recipe for candied orange peel on page 130. You may substitute freshly grated peel if you wish.

A tile in the shape of a honey gingerbread mold.

SCRIPTURE CAKE

Recipes for Scripture cakes, popular in America since colonial days, are riddles to test the cook's knowledge of the Bible.
Each ingredient is indicated by a Biblical reference. "One cup I
Samuel 14:29," for example, refers to the quotation in the First
Book of Samuel, chapter 14, verse 29, "See how my eyes have
become bright, because I tasted a little of this honey." The cook
can tell from this that one cup of honey is called for.

> 4½ cups—I Kings 4:22—flour
> ½ teaspoon—Leviticus 2:13—salt
> 2 tablespoons—Amos 4:5—baking powder
> ½ teaspoon—Chronicles 9:9—ground spices: cinnamon, mace, cloves,
>   allspice, ginger
> ½ cup—Judges—5:25—softened butter
> 1⅓ cup—I Samuel 14:29—honey
> 6—Jeremiah 17:11—eggs
> 2 tablespoons—Judges 4:19—milk
> 2 cups—Nahum 3:12—figs
> 1½ cups—Numbers 17:8—chopped almonds
> 2 cups—I Samuel 30:12—raisins

Preheat oven to 325°.

Sift together the flour, salt, baking powder, and ½ teaspoon
each of cinnamon, mace, cloves, allspice, and ginger. Set aside.

Beat the butter until creamy. Stir in the honey. Then beat in
the eggs, one at a time. Add the milk. Mix well. Stir in the flour
mixture.

Chop the figs. Toss them with 1 tablespoon of flour until
they are lightly coated all over. Add the figs, almonds, and
raisins to the batter. Stir well.

Butter a 10-inch round pan with removable sides. Dust it with flour. Pour in the batter. Bake until a toothpick inserted into the center comes out clean, about 2 hours. Cool completely. Remove the sides of the pan. Wrap cake well with plastic wrap or tinfoil. *One 10-inch cake.*

HONEY JUMBLES
COOKIES

These plain, fragrant, long-lasting cookies are an old English favorite. They should be allowed to ripen for two or three days before eating.

1 tablespoon softened butter	*2 ½ cups flour*
½ cup dark honey	*1 teaspoon baking soda*
½ cup molasses	*½ teaspoon salt*
½ teaspoon vanilla	

Beat the butter until creamy. Stir in the honey and molasses. Add the vanilla.

Mix the flour, baking soda, and salt in a large bowl and beat in the honey mixture. Cover the bowl and let it stand overnight.

Preheat the oven to 350°. Butter a cookie sheet.

Roll teaspoonfuls of dough into balls. Place them 2 inches apart on the cookie sheet. Put the sheet into the oven and bake until the tops of the cookies spring back when lightly touched, about 15 minutes. Remove the cookies with a spatula and cool on racks.

Store the cooled cookies in an airtight container. If they are too hard at first, soften them by adding a slice of peeled apple to the container.   *About 60 cookies.*

HONEY BRAN MUFFINS

Nutritious honey bran muffins can be served with Honey Butter (page 96) or topped with Honey Icing (page 145).

1½ cups whole bran	*1 cup milk*
1½ cups whole wheat flour	*½ cup honey*
1 tablespoon baking powder	*1 egg*
½ teaspoon baking soda	*½ cup softened butter*
1 teaspoon salt	*½ cup raisins*

Preheat the oven to 400°.

Mix together the bran, flour, baking powder, baking soda, and salt in a large bowl. In another bowl, mix together the milk, honey, egg and butter. Beat well. Combine with the bran mixture. Stir in the raisins.

Grease the muffin pans and fill cups two-thirds full. Bake 20 minutes or until done.   *1 dozen muffins.*

A pastry cutter.

Capturing a swarm.

LEKACH
HONEYCAKE

This is a special honeycake that is featured on the Jewish holiday of Rosh Hashana (which means "head of the year") to celebrate the Jewish New Year.

3½ cups flour
½ teaspoon salt
1½ teaspoons baking powder
1½ teaspoons baking soda
½ teaspoon ground cinnamon
½ teaspoon ground nutmeg
½ teaspoon ground cloves

½ teaspoon ground ginger
4 eggs
2½ cups dark honey
3 tablespoons oil
⅓ cup brewed coffee
1½ cups chopped walnuts or almonds

Preheat the oven to 325°.

Sift together the flour, salt, baking powder, baking soda, cinnamon, nutmeg, cloves, and ginger.

Beat the eggs. Beat in the honey. Add the oil and coffee. Mix well. Stir in the flour mixture and the nuts.

Butter two 9-inch loaf pans. Line them with aluminum foil. Butter the foil. Divide the batter equally between the pans. Bake until a toothpick, inserted in the center, comes out clean, about 60-70 minutes. Cool on racks before removing from the pans. Peel off the foil. Wrap well with plastic wrap or tinfoil. *2 loaves.*

ALGERIAN CHARLOTTE

A traditional food of Algeria—dates—is added to a favorite French whipped cream concoction—the charlotte—to make this elegant dessert.

1 cup dates	*2 cups heavy cream*
juice of one orange	*½ cup chopped almonds*
1 ½ cups water	*2 tablespoons sliced almonds*
3 tablespoons honey	*2 chopped dates*
1 tablespoon gelatin	*grated peel of ½ orange*

Remove the pits from the dates. Cut them into quarters and set aside.

Squeeze the orange juice into a saucepan. Add the water and honey. Sprinkle the gelatin onto the mixture. When it dissolves, stir briefly and add the quartered dates. Bring to a boil, reduce the heat, and simmer, covered, 30 minutes. Cool. Strain the mixture and reserve the liquid.

Whip the cream until it stands in peaks. Add the almonds to the date liquid and gently fold it into the cream. Spoon into a two-quart serving dish. Decorate the charlotte with the sliced almonds, chopped dates, and grated orange peel. Chill in the refrigerator for 2 or more hours before serving. *8 to 10 servings.*

SCANDINAVIAN FRUIT SOUP

A refreshing cold soup that may be served as a first course or as a dessert.

1 pound black cherries*   *½ teaspoon whole cloves*
2 cups water   *3 tablespoons cornstarch*
¼ cup honey   *3 tablespoons water*
3 tablespoons lemon juice   *unsweetened yogurt*
1 cinnamon stick

Remove the cherry pits. Put the cherries, 2 cups of water, honey, lemon juice, cinnamon stick, and cloves into a heavy saucepan. Bring to a boil, reduce heat, and simmer until the cherries are tender. Remove the cinnamon stick, press the fruit mixture through a strainer, and return it to the pot.

Mix cornstarch and 3 tablespoons water into a smooth paste. Stir it into the soup and cook, stirring, over low heat until the soup thickens. Cool. Chill in the refrigerator. Serve in individual bowls with a spoonful of unsweetened yogurt.   *4 servings.*

*If fresh cherries are not available, fresh pears may be substituted. Core and quarter them before cooking.

HONEY CUSTARD

Custard is a British favorite. This recipe combines eggs and milk with specially flavored honey to make a simple and nutritious sweet.

2 cups rose* or orange blossom honey   *½ teaspoon salt*
2½ cups milk   *4 eggs*

Preheat the oven to 350°.

Mix the honey, milk, and salt. Stir until smooth.

Beat the eggs. Stir in the honey mixture. Pour into 8 ungreased 5-ounce custard cups. Place the cups on a rack in a shallow pan. Pour ½ inch of hot water into the pan around the cups. Put the pan in the oven and bake until a knife inserted near the edge of a cup comes out clean, about 35 minutes. Cool on racks. Chill in refrigerator for 2 hours or more before serving.

8 servings.

*A recipe for rose honey appears on page 131.

PEANUT BUTTER BALLS

A delicious, high-protein, vitamin-rich snack.

1 cup wheat germ   *2 tablespoons peanuts,*
½ cup peanut butter   *finely chopped*
½ cup honey   *Sesame seeds or coconut*
¼ cup powdered milk

Preheat the oven to 325°.

Spread wheat germ in a shallow pan and bake in the oven, stirring occasionally, until lightly browned, about 10 minutes. Remove and cool.

Mix the wheat germ, peanut butter, honey, and powdered milk. Stir in the chopped peanuts. Form into 1-inch balls. Roll each ball in sesame seeds or coconut until well coated. Refrigerate for two hours or more before serving.

40 peanut butter balls.

HONEY ICING

An unusual icing for cakes and cookies.

1 8-ounce package of cream   *3 tablespoons honey*
cheese   *½ teaspoon vanilla*

Let the cream cheese soften at room temperature for about 45 minutes.

Add honey and vanilla. Blend well with a fork until the mixture is smooth.   *1 cup icing.*

MELI PITA
HONEY PIE

A traditional Greek Easter dessert, which is said to have orig-
inated on the island of Siphnos. The original pie combined
delicious local honey with a special soft cheese made from
sheep's milk.

1 ½ cups flour	*½ cup honey*
½ teaspoon salt	*4 eggs*
½ cup softened butter	*grated rind of 1 lemon*
4 tablespoons cold water	*cinnamon*
1 pound ricotta cheese	

Preheat the oven to 350°.

To make the pie crust, sift together the flour and salt. Add
the butter with a pastry cutter or fork. The mixture will be
crumbly. Gradually add 4 tablespoons of cold water, stirring
until the dough is smooth. Roll out on a floured board with a

rolling pin. Lift the dough carefully into a 9-inch pie plate. Pat into place and trim the edges. Set aside.

Beat the cheese and honey together. Add the eggs, one at a time, beating after each addition. Grate the lemon rind and stir it into the cheese mixture. Pour the mixture into the pie crust. Bake until a knife inserted in the center comes out clean, about 50 minutes. Cool. Sprinkle with cinnamon. Chill in the refrigerator. *6 to 8 servings.*

AISH-EL-SARAYA
EGYPTIAN PALACE BREAD

A rich, chewy, butterscotch-flavored variation on the traditional bread-and-butter pudding. This wonderful dessert takes only a few minutes to prepare.

8 slices white bread	*½ cup butter*
1 cup light honey	*1 cup heavy cream*

Cut the crusts off the bread and crumble it.

Heat the honey in a heavy skillet until it comes to a boil. Be careful that the honey does not boil over. Add the butter and crumbled bread. Reduce the heat and simmer, stirring, until the mixture forms a thick paste, about 5 minutes.

Pour the paste into a shallow serving dish. Chill in the refrigerator for 1 hour or more. Pour the cream over the top and serve.

4 servings.

FRUIT COMPOTE

A wholesome fruit dessert that is easily prepared and nicely flavored with lemon and orange.

1 pound mixed dried apricots,   *½ cup honey*
  apples, and peaches   *1 lemon*
1 cup raisins   *1 orange*
4 cups water

Preheat the oven to 275°.

Put the dried fruit, raisins, and water into a shallow baking dish. Place in the oven and bake 1½ hours. Remove from the oven and stir in the honey, being careful not to tear the fruit.

Slice the lemon and orange. Gently stir into the cooked fruit. Return to the oven and bake 30 minutes longer. Serve hot or cold.

6 to 8 servings.

SPICY ORANGES

These spicy oranges make a refreshing dish by themselves. Or they can be mixed with slices of banana, fresh melon, and berries in a tasty fruit cocktail.

2 tablespoons fresh lemon juice   *¼ cup honey*
⅛ teaspoon ground cinnamon   *6 oranges*
⅛ teaspoon ground cloves

Mix the lemon juice, cinnamon, cloves, and honey in a small saucepan. Cook over medium heat until the mixture comes to a boil. Boil 1 minute. Be sure that the mixture does not boil over. Remove from the heat and set aside.

Peel the oranges. Separate the sections and remove any pits. Place the sections in a bowl and pour the honey mixture on top. Stir gently until all the orange sections are coated. Chill before serving.   *4 to 6 servings.*

Speaking of Honey

SUCH WORDS as *honey, mead, bee, drone,* and *queen* may seem simple and straightforward. But scholars of language have revealed that there is more here than meets the eye—and that sometimes the ear can tell us more.

The vocabulary of honey is interesting because it is so very old. In fact, it is part of the original group of words with which most of the major languages of the world began. These languages—including such widely scattered tongues as English, Hindi, Greek, Latin, Gaelic, and Russian—are known as the Indo-European family, because all of them are descended from a lost language called Indo-European.

Who were the speakers of Indo-European? Where did they live, and when? Nobody knows. But the modern languages that descended from Indo-European tell us a great deal about these people. And one thing we know for certain is that bees and honey were part of their life.

The English word *honey* closely resembles the German word *honig* and the Dutch *honing*. But other beekeeping terms are even more interesting. They show connections between English and many other languages, some quite distantly related.

Mead, the alcoholic drink made from honey, is a perfect example. We can tell mead was enjoyed all through Europe and Asia. The word for mead is *mjod* in Russian, *mjöd* in Swedish, *miodh* in Irish, and *madh* in Hindi.

The word for *bee* shows more variation, because different languages refer to different features of the bee. Sometimes the word means "honey-maker," sometimes it means "stinger," and sometimes it means "buzzer." In many languages, the word for bee was meant to imitate the sound the insect makes. Examples include the German *biene*, Gaelic *beach*—and English *bee* itself.

The English word *drone* and most of its cousins in other languages are also meant to be imitations of a sound—the drone is called that because it makes the loudest droning noise in the hive. In some languages the imitation is similar to the English one—for instance, Norwegian *drone* and German *drohne*. In others, the attempt at imitation is different. An example is the Spanish *zángano*, which sounds unmistakably like a loud buzz.

Of course, not every beekeeping word is an old one. In fact, every word referring to the queen bee is relatively new. This is due to an advance in scientific knowlege. Until a few hundred years ago, the queen bee's role in the hive was not understood, and she was generally referred to as the king bee.

SELECTED BIBLIOGRAPHY

Beck, Bodog F. and Doree Smedley. *Honey and Your Health*. New York: Dodd, Mead and Company, 1948.

Agricultural Research Service. *Beekeeping in the United States*. Agricultural Handbook Number 335. rev. ed. Washington, D.C.: U.S. Department of Agriculture, June, 1971.

Bodenheimer, F. S. *Insects as Human Food*. The Hague: Dr. W. Junk, Publishers, 1951.

Butler, Charles. *The Feminine Monarchie; or, The Historie of Bees*. London: Printed by I. Haviland for R. Jackson, 1623.

Center for Disease Control. "Honey and Infant Botulism." *Morbidity and Mortality Weekly Report*, 27 (1978): 249–255.

Cosman, Madeline Pelner. *Fabulous Feasts*. New York: George Braziller, Inc.,1976.

Edwardes, Tickner. *The Lore of the Honeybee*. London: Methuen & Co., Ltd., 1908.

Elkon, Juliette. *The Honey Cookbook*. New York: Alfred A. Knopf, 1963.

Flower, Barbara and Elizabeth Rosenbaum. *The Roman Cookery Book (A Critical Translation of the* Art of Cooking, *by Apicius)*. London: George Harrap and Co., Ltd., 1958.

Fraser, H. Malcolm. *Beekeeping in Antiquity*. London: University of London Press, Ltd., 1931.

Friedman, Herbert. *The Honey Guides*. United States National Museum Bulletin 208. Washington, D.C.: Smithsonian Institute, 1955.

Gayre, G. R. *Wassail! In Mazers of Mead*. London: Philmore and Co., Ltd., 1948.

Herrod-Hempsall, William. *Beekeeping New and Old*. Vols. I and II. London: The British Bee Journal, 1937.

The Hive and The Honeybee. Edited by Dadant and Sons. Hamilton, Illinois: Dadant and Sons, 1975.

Honey: A Comprehensive Survey. Edited by Eva Crane. London: William Heinemann, Ltd., 1975.

Jarvis, D. C. *Folk Medicine*. New York: Holt, Rinehart and Winston, Inc., 1958.

Larson, Peggy Pickering and Marvin W. Larson. *Lives of Social Insects.* New York and Cleveland: The World Publishing Company, 1968.

LeSage, D. E. "Bees in Indo-European Languages." *Bee World,* 55 (1974): 15–26, 46–52.

Maeterlinck, Maurice. *The Life of the Bee.* New York: Dodd, Mead and Company, 1904.

Mayer, Jean. *A Diet for Living.* New York: David McKay Company, Inc., 1975.

Milton, John. *Milton's Practical Beekeeper.* London: John W. Parker, 1843.

Ransome, Hilda M. *The Sacred Bee.* Boston and New York: Houghton Mifflin Company, 1937.

Root, A. I. *The ABC and XYZ of Bee Culture.* Medina, Ohio: The A. I. Root Company, 1975.

Stadtlaender, Chris. *Honey Cookery.* London: Thorsons Publishers, Ltd., 1967.

Tannahill, Reay. *Food in History.* New York: Stein and Day Publishers, 1973.

Teale, Edwin Way. *The Golden Throng.* New York: Dodd, Mead and Company, 1961.

Tonsley, Cecil. *Honey for Health.* New York: Award Books, 1969.

Two Fifteenth Century Cookery Books. Edited by Thomas Austin. London: Published by N. Trübner and Company for the Early English Text Society, 1888.

von Frisch, Karl. *Bees: Their Vision, Chemical Senses, and Language.* Ithaca and London: Cornell University Press, 1971.

———. *The Dance, Language, and Orientation of Bees.* Cambridge, Massachusetts: The Belknap Press of Harvard University Press, 1967.

Wilson, Edward O. *The Insect Societies.* Cambridge, Massachusetts: The Belknap Press of Harvard University Press, 1971.

INDEX

Ackersegam, 79
Andaman Island, 46
Africa, 46
Alexander the Great, 71
alfalfa honey, 83
Algeria, 142
America, 44
antiseptic qualities of honey, 13
ants, 39, 41, 63
aphids, 37, 39
Apicius, 100
Arabs, 16, 54
Asia, 35, 36
Athol Brose (liquor), 70
Australia, 36, 41
avocado, 83

Babylon, 78, 93
basil, 79
bears, 63
beehive; ancient Greek, 57; care of by
    workers, 28, 29; development of,
    57; early, man-made, 52, 56; in
    Egypt, 54; in Middle Ages, 57;
    modern, 57-60; population of, 27
beekeeping; development of, 52, 54;
    Zeidler (German), 45; modern,
    58-61; origin, 49, 52; problems of,
    61, 63, 64, 65, 73
beeline, 43, 44
"bee space", 57
bee sting, 43
bee, stingless, 36, 37
bees, (see also queen, drone, workers);
    behavior system, 25; brought to
    America, 65, 68; communication by
    dancing, 33, 34; derivation of word,
    152; detecting nectar, 32; eyesight
    of, 32; flight speed, 44; hearing of,

55; hives (see beehive); homing flight
    of, 43, 44; life cycle, 27-29; myths
    about, 13, 25, 26, 54, 55; nests,
    43-45, 47, 81; predators on, 63, 64;
    reproduction of, 25-28; species of,
    35, 36; as symbols, 54
bees' nest, 43-45, 47, 48, 81
bees' wax, 32, 47, 59, 85
Benner, Dr. Bircher, 117
Bible, 39, 80-82, 136
Book of Mormon, 82
British Royal Air Force, 21
bumble bee, life style, 21
buckwheat honey, 83

Caesar, Julius, 84
Cairo, 54
Center for Disease Control, 21
Charles I, 23
charoses, 81, 126, 127
chemical components of honey, 18-21
China, 16
chunk honey, 86
clover honey, 83
comb honey, see also honeycomb; eat-
    ing, 84, 85; grades of, 87; varieties
    of, 85, 86
cooking with honey, hints on, 92, 93,
    96
cosmetics using honey, 71, 73-75
cough syrup, 18

Deseret, 82
dextrose, 20
Dijon, 134
"domesticated bees," 49
Drambuie (liquor), 70
drone; function, 27, 28; word deriva-
    tion, 152

RECIPE INDEX

[159]